Ninja Foodi Digital Air Fry Oven Complete Cookbook

Easy & Amazing Air Crisp, Air Broil, Bake, Dehydrate, Toast, and More Recipes for Beginners and Advanced Users

Martha Rhea

© Copyright 2020 - All rights reserved.

The content contained within this book may not be reproduced, duplicated or transmitted without direct written permission from the author or the publisher.

Under no circumstances will any blame or legal responsibility be held against the publisher, or author, for any damages, reparation, or monetary loss due to the information contained within this book, either directly or indirectly.

Legal Notice:

This book is copyright protected. It is only for personal use. You cannot amend, distribute, sell, use, quote or paraphrase any part, or the content within this book, without the consent of the author or publisher.

Disclaimer Notice:

Please note the information contained within this document is for educational and entertainment purposes only. All effort has been executed to present accurate, up to date, reliable, complete information. No warranties of any kind are declared or implied. Readers acknowledge that the author is not engaged in the rendering of legal, financial, medical or professional advice. The content within this book has been derived from various sources. Please consult a licensed professional before attempting any techniques outlined in this book.

By reading this document, the reader agrees that under no circumstances is the author responsible for any losses, direct or indirect, that are incurred as a result of the use of the information contained within this document, including, but not limited to, errors, omissions, or inaccuracies.

Table of Contents

Introduction..................................5
- What is Ninja Foodi Digital Air Fry Oven?......6
- Tips to use Ninja Foodi Digital Air Fry Oven. 7

Breakfast Recipes........................8
- Egg & Potato Hash 8
- Eggs in Avocado Cups........................ 9
- Banana Bread 10
- Chicken & Zucchini Omelet 11
- Eggs in Bread Cups.......................... 12
- Bacon & Spinach Muffins 13
- Cinnamon French Toasts 14
- Tomato Quiche 15
- Ham & Hash Brown Casserole................ 16
- Spinach & Tomato Frittata 17

Snacks & Appetizer Recipes 18
- Chili Dip 18
- Salmon Croquettes 19
- Crispy Coconut Prawns 20
- Buffalo Chicken Wings 21
- Spicy Chickpeas 22
- Cheese Pastries 23
- Mozzarella Sticks 24
- Jalapeño Poppers 25
- Cheddar Biscuits 26
- French Fries.................................27

Poultry Recipes 28
- Marinated Chicken Thighs 28
- Thyme Duck Breast 29
- Glazed Turkey Breast........................30
- Breaded Chicken Breast 31
- Garlicky Duck Legs 32
- Herbed Chicken Drumsticks..................33
- Lemony Turkey Legs 34
- Chicken Cordon Bleu 35
- Spiced Chicken Thighs 36
- Glazed Chicken Drumsticks..................37
- Herbed Roasted Chicken 38
- Herbed Turkey Breast 39
- Roasted Cornish Game Hen 40
- Spicy Chicken Legs 41
- Rosemary Chicken Thighs 42
- Bacon-Wrapped Chicken Breasts 43

Beef, Pork & Lamb Recipes 44
- Glazed Lamb Meatballs 44
- Spiced Flank Steak 45
- Pork Meatloaf 46
- Glazed Pork Tenderloin 47
- Buttered Leg of Lamb........................48

Herbed Pork Chops 49

Glazed Lamb Chops 50

Stuffed Pork Roll 51

Almonds Crusted Rack of Lamb 52

Buttered Rib-Eye Steak 53

Bacon-Wrapped Filet Mignon 54

Beef Sirloin Roast 55

Fish and Seafood 56

Crab Rangoon 56

Lobster Tail 57

Baked Salmon 58

Crusted Tilapia 59

Shrimp and Crab Casserole 60

Lemon Shrimp and Vegetables 61

Garlic Parmesan Shrimp 62

Mangalorean Fish Fry 63

Bacon Wrapped Shrimp 64

Cajun Shrimp 65

Sheet Pan Shrimp Asparagus Potato 66

Vegetables and Sides 67

Kale and Potato Nuggets 67

Loaded Tater Tots 68

Eggplant Parmesan 69

Tofu Butternut Squash Dinner 70

Sheet Pan Tofu Dinner 71

Spicy Cauliflower Stir-Fry 72

Porcini Mac and Cheese 73

Herbed Potato, Asparagus, and Chickpea 74

Kale Salad with Roasted Veggies 75

Sheet Pan Fajitas 76

Artichoke Spinach Casserole 77

Dessert Recipes 78

Molten Lava Cake 78

Sweet Apples 79

Carrot Cake 80

Strawberry Roll Cake 81

Bread Pudding 82

French Toast Sticks with Berries 83

Fudgy Brownies 84

Glazed Donut 85

Cinnamon Rolls 86

Crispy Oreos 87

3 Weeks Meal Plan: 88

Week 1 88

Week 2 89

Week 3 91

Conclusion 93

Introduction

We all need a kitchen appliance that can make our lives easy and give us a well cooked, healthy meal every time. here we bring you just the device that will meet all your cooking needs and will help you make delicious food with minimum efforts and time, the Ninja Foodi Digital Air Fry Oven!

With the new Ninja Foodi Digital Air Fry oven, you can get to bake, Air fry roast, toast, broil and dehydrate all in a single place. Its advanced digital technology saves both your energy and efforts. The Ninja Foodi cooking series stands apart from other electric appliances due to the multitude of benefits they guarantee in a single device. The Ninja Food Air Fry Oven is not only a good cooker but it's unique built makes it perfect for cooking all serving sizes.

What is Ninja Foodi Digital Air Fry Oven?

The Ninja Digital Air Fry oven has made it possible for every user to cook and enjoy fresh and crispy meals in no time. It is an electric oven that has merged with other smart cooking features like Air Frying, broiling, roasting, toasting, and dehydrating. This appliance is especially good for people who love to bake and cook crispy food. When you buy the 8 in 1 Ninja Air Fry oven SP101, here is what you are going in to get inside the box:

- The Ninja Digital Air Fry oven main unit with the flip design
- An Air Fry basket
- A Roast tray
- A Sheet pan
- A removable crumb tray

Unlike conventional oven or Air Fryers, the Ninja Foodi digital Air Fry oven comes with an adjustable space feature, which means that you can place the oven both horizontally and vertically over the kitchen shelf. For cooking, the oven can be placed in its horizontal position. And when not in use, the cleaned oven can be flipped to stand vertically on the shelf. This creates an extra space over the shelf without doing much. Just make sure to flip the oven only when it is completely cooled and clean.

This Air Fry oven comes with 8 functions in one. A user can Air Fryer, Air Roast, bake, toast bread and bagel, dehydrate and broil food just on a press of a button. You can also switch from one mode to another during the cooking if needed. The toast and bagel function give you options to select the darkness of the bread as desired.

Tips to use Ninja Foodi Digital Air Fry Oven

If you are completely new to this appliance, then here is how you can cook using its different cooking functions:

1. First, check all the components of the appliance and see if they all intact and in good shape.
2. To use the appliance for the first time, clean or wash its cooking accessories like the baking pan, sheet pan, and Air Fryer basket and let them completely dry.
3. Now plug in the device and press the "Power button" given on the control panel.
4. After pressing this button, the LED will light up and indicate the device is one.
5. Place the crumb tray at the bottom of the oven.
6. The Ninja Foodi digital Air Fry oven quickly preheats itself, so it is recommended to place the food inside and then set the mode, time, and temperature accordingly. Or at least keep the food ready to place inside the oven when it is preheated.
7. Place the prepared food inside and close the lid or door of the Ninja Foodi digital Air Fry oven.
8. To do so, first select the cooking mode. Rotate the dial, and it will switch between the modes. Stop rotating the dial when the blue light appears beside your desired mode.
9. After selecting the function, it's time to change the temperature and time settings.
10. To change the cooking time, first press the "Time" button and then rotate the dial to increase or decrease the number of minutes.
11. Similarly, to change the temperature, press the "Temp" button and rotate the dial to adjust the temperature according.
12. It is to note here that the "Time" button is also used to select the number of "Slices" when the oven is running on the "Toast" and "Bagel" mode, and the "Temp" button is used to set the level of "darkness" of the toasts on the given modes.
13. Initiate Cooking:
14. When the mode, temp, and time are adjusted, the device is ready to use.
15. For Baking, Air Frying, Air Roasting, and Broiling, the device takes some time to preheat.
16. It starts to preheat when the Dial is pressed to start the cooking.
17. At this point, the Led screen will show PRE in red color, and the timer does not start ticking until the PRE sign disappears and the device is preheated.
18. Once it is preheated, the device beeps to indicate that it will now automatically start cooking, and its timer will start running.
19. When the food is cooked, the device keeps it warm until you are ready to remove it from the oven.

Breakfast Recipes

Egg & Potato Hash

Preparation Time: 10 minutes
Cooking Time: 20 minutes
Servings: 1

Ingredients:

- 2 bacon slices, halved
- 2 small potatoes, chopped
- ¼ of tomato, chopped
- 1 egg
- 2 tablespoons cheddar cheese, shredded

Preparation:

1. Arrange the bacon strips onto a double layer of tin foil.
2. Place the potatoes and tomato n top of the bacon.
3. Carefully crack the egg on top of the veggie mixture.
4. With the tin foil, shape the mixture into a bowl.
5. Press "Power Button" of Ninja Foodi Digital Air Fry Oven and turn the dial to select "Air Roast" mode.
6. Press "Time Button" and again turn the dial to set the cooking time to 20 minutes.
7. Now push "Temp Button" and rotate the dial to set the temperature at 350 degrees F.
8. Press "Start/Pause" button to start.
9. When the unit beeps to show that it is preheated, open the lid.
10. Carefully arrange the foil piece over the wire rack and insert in the oven.
11. After 16 minutes of cooking, top the hash with cheese.
12. When cooking time is complete, open the lid and transfer the foil pieces onto serving plates.
13. Serve hot.

Serving Suggestions: Garnishing of fresh parsley will enhance the taste of this potato hash.

Variation Tip: Use the right kind of potatoes.

Nutritional Information per Serving:

Calories: 326|**Fat:** 13.4g|**Sat Fat:** 5.9g|**Carbohydrates:** 36.8g|**Fiber:** 5.6g|**Sugar:** 3.4g|**Protein:** 15.9g

Eggs in Avocado Cups

Preparation Time: 10 minutes
Cooking Time: 10 minutes
Servings: 2

Ingredients:

- 1 avocado, halved and pitted
- 2 large eggs
- Salt and freshly ground black pepper, to taste
- 2 cooked bacon slices, crumbled

Preparation:

1. Carefully scoop out about 2 teaspoons of flesh from each avocado half.
2. Crack 1 egg in each avocado half and sprinkle with salt and black pepper lightly.
3. Arrange avocado halves onto the greased piece of foil-lined sheet pan.
4. Press "Power Button" of Ninja Foodi Digital Air Fry Oven and turn the dial to select "Air Roast" mode.
5. Press "Time Button" and again turn the dial to set the cooking time to 10 minutes.
6. Now push "Temp Button" and rotate the dial to set the temperature at 375 degrees F.
7. Press "Start/Pause" button to start.
8. When the unit beeps to show that it is preheated, open the lid and insert the sheet pan in the oven.
9. When cooking time is complete, open the lid and transfer the avocado halves onto serving plates.
10. Top each avocado half with bacon pieces and serve.

Serving Suggestions: Serve these avocado halves with cherry tomatoes and fresh spinach.

Variation Tip: Smoked salmon can be replaced with bacon too.

Nutritional Information per Serving:

Calories: 300|**Fat:** 26.6g|**Sat Fat:** 6.4g|**Carbohydrates:** 9g|**Fiber:** 6.7g|**Sugar:** 0.9g|**Protein:** 9.7g

Banana Bread

Preparation Time: 15 minutes
Cooking Time: 40 minutes
Servings: 6

Ingredients:

- 1½ cups cake flour
- 1 teaspoon baking soda
- ½ teaspoon ground cinnamon
- Salt, to taste
- ½ cup vegetable oil
- 2 eggs
- ½ cup sugar
- ½ teaspoon vanilla extract
- 3 medium bananas, peeled and mashed
- ½ cup raisins, chopped finely

Preparation:

1. In a large bowl, mix together the flour, baking soda, cinnamon, and salt.
2. In another bowl, beat well eggs and oil.
3. Add the sugar, vanilla extract, and bananas and beat until well combined.
4. Add the flour mixture and stir until just combined.
5. Place the mixture into a lightly greased baking pan and sprinkle with raisins
6. With a piece of foil, cover the pan loosely.
7. Press "Power Button" of Ninja Foodi Digital Air Fry Oven and turn the dial to select "Air Bake" mode.
8. Press "Time Button" and again turn the dial to set the cooking time to 30 minutes.
9. Now push "Temp Button" and rotate the dial to set the temperature at 300 degrees F.
10. Press "Start/Pause" button to start.
11. When the unit beeps to show that it is preheated, open the lid.
12. Arrange the pan into the air fry basket and insert in the oven.
13. After 30 minutes of cooking, set the temperature to 285 degrees F for 10 minutes.
14. When cooking time is complete, open the lid and place the pan onto a wire rack to cool for about 10 minutes.
15. Carefully invert the bread onto the wire rack to cool completely before slicing.
16. Cut the bread into desired-sized slices and serve.

Serving Suggestions: Any kind of fruit jam will be great with this bread.

Variation Tip: Don't overmix the mixture.

Nutritional Information per Serving:

Calories: 448|**Fat:** 20.2g|**Sat Fat:** 4.1g|**Carbohydrates:** 63.9g|**Fiber:** 2.9g|**Sugar:** 31.3g|**Protein:** 6.1g

Chicken & Zucchini Omelet

Preparation Time: 15 minutes
Cooking Time: 35 minutes
Servings: 6

Ingredients:

- 8 eggs
- ½ cup milk
- Salt and freshly ground black pepper, to taste
- 1 cup cooked chicken, chopped
- 1 cup Cheddar cheese, shredded
- ½ cup fresh chives, chopped
- ¾ cup zucchini, chopped

Preparation:

1. In a bowl, add the eggs, milk, salt and black pepper and beat well.
2. Add the remaining ingredients and stir to combine.
3. Place the mixture into a greased baking pan.
4. Press "Power Button" of Ninja Foodi Digital Air Fry Oven and turn the dial to select "Air Bake" mode.
5. Press "Time Button" and again turn the dial to set the cooking time to 35 minutes.
6. Now push "Temp Button" and rotate the dial to set the temperature at 315 degrees F.
7. Press "Start/Pause" button to start.
8. When the unit beeps to show that it is preheated, open the lid.
9. Arrange pan over the wire rack and insert in the oven.
10. When cooking time is complete, open the lid and place the baking pan aside for about 5 minutes.
11. Cut into equal-sized wedges and serve hot.

Serving Suggestions: Toasted bread slices will go great with this omelet.

Variation Tip: You can stuff this omelet with any cooked meat like turkey, bacon, crab oe sausage.

Nutritional Information per Serving:

Calories: 209|**Fat:** 13.3g|**Sat Fat:** 6.3g|**Carbohydrates:** 2.3g|**Fiber:** 0.3g|**Sugar:** 1.8g|**Protein:** 9.8g

Eggs in Bread Cups

Preparation Time: 10 minutes
Cooking Time: 23 minutes
Servings: 4

Ingredients:

- 4 bacon slices
- 2 bread slices, crust removed
- 4 eggs
- Salt and freshly ground black pepper, to taste

Preparation:

1. Grease 4 cups of a muffin tin and set aside.
2. Heat a small frying pan over medium-high heat and cook the bacon slices for about 2-3 minutes.
3. With a slotted spoon, transfer the bacon slice onto a paper towel-lined plate to cool.
4. Break each bread slice in half.
5. Arrange 1 bread slices half in each of the prepared muffin cup and press slightly.
6. Now, arrange 1 bacon slice over each bread slice in a circular shape.
7. Crack 1 egg into each muffin cup and sprinkle with salt and black pepper.
8. Press "Power Button" of Ninja Foodi Digital Air Fry Oven and turn the dial to select "Air Bake" mode.
9. Press "Time Button" and again turn the dial to set the cooking time to 20 minutes.
10. Now push "Temp Button" and rotate the dial to set the temperature at 350 degrees F.
11. Press "Start/Pause" button to start.
12. When the unit beeps to show that it is preheated, open the lid.
13. Arrange the muffin tin over the wire rack and insert in the oven.
14. When cooking time is complete, open the lid and place the muffin tin onto a wire rack for about 10 minutes.
15. Serve warm.

Serving Suggestions: Feel free to top the bread cups with fresh herbs of your choice before serving.

Variation Tip: Pancetta can be used instead of bacon.

Nutritional Information per Serving:

Calories: 98|**Fat:** 6.6g|**Sat Fat:** 2.1g|**Carbohydrates:** 2.6g|**Fiber:** 0.1g|**Sugar:** 0.5g|**Protein:** 7.3g

Bacon & Spinach Muffins

Preparation Time: 10 minutes
Cooking Time: 17 minutes
Servings: 6

Ingredients:

- 6 eggs
- ½ cup milk
- Salt and freshly ground black pepper, to taste
- 1 cup fresh spinach, chopped
- 4 cooked bacon slices, crumbled

Preparation:

1. In a bowl, add the eggs, milk, salt and black pepper and beat until well combined.
2. Add the spinach and stir to combine.
3. Divide the spinach mixture into 6 greased cups of an egg bite mold evenly.
4. Press "Power Button" of Ninja Foodi Digital Air Fry Oven and turn the dial to select "Air Fry" mode.
5. Press "Time Button" and again turn the dial to set the cooking time to 17 minutes.
6. Now push "Temp Button" and rotate the dial to set the temperature at 325 degrees F.
7. Press "Start/Pause" button to start.
8. When the unit beeps to show that it is preheated, open the lid.
9. Arrange the mold over the wire rack and insert in the oven.
10. When cooking time is complete, open the lid and place the mold onto a wire rack to cool for about 5 minutes.
11. Top with bacon pieces and serve warm.

Serving Suggestions: Serve these muffins with the drizzling of melted butter.

Variation Tip: Don't forget to grease the egg bite molds before pacing the egg mixture in them.

Nutritional Information per Serving:

Calories: 179|**Fat:** 12.9g|**Sat Fat:** 4.3g|**Carbohydrates:** 1.8g|**Fiber:** 0.1g|**Sugar:** 1.3g|**Protein:** 13.5g

Cinnamon French Toasts

Preparation Time: 10 minutes
Cooking Time: 5 minutes
Servings: 2

Ingredients:

- 2 eggs
- ¼ cup whole milk
- 3 tablespoons sugar
- 2 teaspoons olive oil
- 1/8 teaspoon vanilla extract
- 1/8 teaspoon ground cinnamon
- 4 bread slices

Preparation:

1. In a large bowl, add all the ingredients except for bread slices and mix well.
2. Coat the bread slices with egg mixture evenly.
3. Press "Power Button" of Ninja Foodi Digital Air Fry Oven and turn the dial to select "Air Fry" mode.
4. Press "Time Button" and again turn the dial to set the cooking time to 6 minutes.
5. Now push "Temp Button" and rotate the dial to set the temperature at 390 degrees F.
6. Press "Start/Pause" button to start.
7. When the unit beeps to show that it is preheated, open the lid and lightly grease the sheet pan.
8. Arrange the bread slices into the air fry basket and insert in the oven.
9. Flip the bread slices once halfway through.
10. When cooking time is complete, open the lid and transfer the French toast onto serving plates.
11. Serve warm.

Serving Suggestions: You can enjoy these French toast with the drizzling of maple syrup.

Variation Tip: For best result, soak the bread slices in egg mixture until each slice is thoroughly saturated.

Nutritional Information per Serving:

Calories: 238|**Fat:** 10.6g|**Sat Fat:** 2.7g|**Carbohydrates:** 20.8g|**Fiber:** 0.5g|**Sugar:** 0.9g|**Protein:** 7.9g

Tomato Quiche

Preparation Time: 10 minutes
Cooking Time: 30 minutes
Servings: 2

Ingredients:

- 4 eggs
- ¼ cup onion, chopped
- ½ cup tomatoes, chopped
- ½ cup milk
- 1 cup Gouda cheese, shredded
- Salt, to taste

Preparation:

1. In a small baking pan, add all the ingredients and mix well.
2. Press "Power Button" of Ninja Foodi Digital Air Fry Oven and turn the dial to select "Air Fry" mode.
3. Press "Time Button" and again turn the dial to set the cooking time to 30 minutes.
4. Now push "Temp Button" and rotate the dial to set the temperature at 340 degrees F.
5. Press "Start/Pause" button to start.
6. When the unit beeps to show that it is preheated, open the lid.
7. Arrange the pan over the wire rack and insert in the oven.
8. When cooking time is complete, open the lid and place the pan aside for about 5 minutes.
9. Cut into equal-sized wedges and serve.

Serving Suggestions: Fresh baby spring mix will be a great companion for this quiche.

Variation Tip: You can use any kind of fresh veggies for the filling of quiche.

Nutritional Information per Serving:

Calories: 247|**Fat:** 16.1g|**Sat Fat:** 7.5g|**Carbohydrates:** 7.3g|**Fiber:** 0.9g|**Sugar:** 5.2g|**Protein:** 18.6g

Ham & Hash Brown Casserole

Preparation Time: 15 minutes
Cooking Time: 35 minutes
Servings: 5

Ingredients:

- 1½ tablespoons olive oil
- ½ of large onion, chopped
- 24 ounces frozen hash browns
- 3 eggs
- 2 tablespoons milk
- Salt and freshly ground black pepper, to taste
- ½ pound ham, chopped
- ¼ cup Cheddar cheese, shredded

Preparation:

1. In a skillet, heat the oil over medium heat and sauté the onion for about 4-5 minutes.
2. Remove from the heat and transfer the onion into a bowl.
3. Add the hash browns and mix well.
4. Place the mixture into a baking pan.
5. Press "Power Button" of Ninja Foodi Digital Air Fry Oven and turn the dial to select "Air Bake" mode.
6. Press "Time Button" and again turn the dial to set the cooking time to 32 minutes.
7. Now push "Temp Button" and rotate the dial to set the temperature at 350 degrees F.
8. Press "Start/Pause" button to start.
9. When the unit beeps to show that it is preheated, open the lid.
10. Arrange pan over the wire rack and insert in the oven.
11. Stir the mixture once after 8 minutes.
12. Meanwhile, in a bowl, add the eggs, milk, salt and black pepper and beat well.
13. After 15 minutes of cooking, place the egg mixture over hash brown mixture evenly and top with the ham.
14. After 30 minutes of cooking, sprinkle the casserole with the cheese.
15. When cooking time is complete, open the lid and place the casserole dish aside for about 5 minutes.
16. Cut into equal-sized wedges and serve.

Serving Suggestions: Avocado slices will accompany this casserole greatly.

Variation Tip: Use freshly shredded cheese.

Nutritional Information per Serving:

Calories: 540|**Fat:** 29.8g|**Sat Fat:** 6.5g|**Carbohydrates:** 51.5g|**Fiber:** 5.3g|**Sugar:** 3.2g|**Protein:** 16.7g

Spinach & Tomato Frittata

Preparation Time: 15 minutes
Cooking Time: 30 minutes
Servings: 6

Ingredients:

- 10 large eggs
- Salt and freshly ground black pepper, to taste
- 1 (5-ounce) bag baby spinach
- 2 cups grape tomatoes, halved
- 4 scallions, sliced thinly
- 8 ounces feta cheese, crumbled
- 3 tablespoons hot olive oil

Preparation:

1. In a bowl, place the eggs, salt and black pepper and beat well.
2. Add the spinach, tomatoes, scallions and feta cheese and gently stir to combine.
3. Spread the oil in a baking pan and top with the spinach mixture.
4. Press "Power Button" of Ninja Foodi Digital Air Fry Oven and turn the dial to select "Air Bake" mode.
5. Press "Time Button" and again turn the dial to set the cooking time to 30 minutes.
6. Now push "Temp Button" and rotate the dial to set the temperature at 350 degrees F.
7. Press "Start/Pause" button to start.
8. When the unit beeps to show that it is preheated, open the lid.
9. Arrange pan over the wire rack and insert in the oven.
10. When cooking time is complete, open the lid and place the pan aside for about 5 minutes.
11. Cut into equal-sized wedges and serve hot.

Serving Suggestions: Enjoy your frittata with garlicky potatoes.

Variation Tip: Pick the right cheese for frittata.

Nutritional Information per Serving:

Calories: 298|**Fat:** 23.6g|**Sat Fat:** 9.3g|**Carbohydrates:** 6.1g|**Fiber:** 1.5g|**Sugar:** 4.1g|**Protein:** 17.2g

Snacks & Appetizer Recipes

Chili Dip

Preparation Time: 10 minutes
Cooking Time: 15 minutes
Servings: 8

Ingredients:

- 1 (8-ounce) package cream cheese, softened
- 1 (16-ounce) can Hormel chili without beans
- 1 (16-ounce) package mild cheddar cheese, shredded

Preparation:

1. In a baking pan, place the cream cheese and spread in an even layer.
2. Top with chili evenly, followed by the cheese.
3. Press "Power Button" of Ninja Foodi Digital Air Fry Oven and turn the dial to select "Air Bake" mode.
4. Press "Time Button" and again turn the dial to set the cooking time to 15 minutes.
5. Now push "Temp Button" and rotate the dial to set the temperature at 375 degrees F.
6. Press "Start/Pause" button to start.
7. When the unit beeps to show that it is preheated, open the lid.
8. Arrange pan over the wire rack and insert in the oven.
9. When cooking time is complete, open the lid.
10. Serve hot.

Serving Suggestions: serve this dip with tortilla chips or fresh veggies.

Variation Tip: Coby cheese can be replaced with cheddar cheese.

Nutritional Information per Serving:

Calories: 388|**Fat:** 31.3g|**Sat Fat:** 19.2g|**Carbohydrates:** 5.6g|**Fiber:** 0.7g|**Sugar:** 1.1g|**Protein:** 21.1g

Salmon Croquettes

Preparation Time: 15 minutes
Cooking Time: 7 minutes
Servings: 8

Ingredients:

- ½ of large can red salmon, drained
- 1 egg, lightly beaten
- 1 tablespoon fresh parsley, chopped
- Salt and freshly ground black pepper, to taste
- 3 tablespoons vegetable oil
- ½ cup breadcrumbs

Preparation:

1. In a bowl, add the salmon and with a fork, mash it completely.
2. Add the eggs, parsley, salt, and black pepper and mix until well combined.
3. Make 8 equal-sized croquettes from the mixture.
4. In a shallow dish, mix together the oil and breadcrumbs.
5. Coat the croquettes with the breadcrumb mixture.
6. Press "Power Button" of Ninja Foodi Digital Air Fry Oven and turn the dial to select "Air Fry" mode.
7. Press "Time Button" and again turn the dial to set the cooking time to 7 minutes.
8. Now push "Temp Button" and rotate the dial to set the temperature at 390 degrees F.
9. Press "Start/Pause" button to start.
10. When the unit beeps to show that it is preheated, open the lid.
11. Arrange the croquettes in the air fry basket and insert in the oven. When cooking time is complete, open the lid and transfer the croquettes onto a platter.
12. Serve warm.

Serving Suggestions: These croquettes will be great with any kind of dipping sauce.

Variation Tip: Strictly follow the ratio of ingredients.

Nutritional Information per Serving:

Calories: 117|**Fat:** 7.8g|**Sat Fat:** 1.5g|**Carbohydrates:** 4.9g|**Fiber:** 0.3g|**Sugar:** 0.5g|**Protein:** 7.1g

Crispy Coconut Prawns

Preparation Time: 20 minutes
Cooking Time: 12 minutes
Servings: 4

Ingredients:

- ½ cup flour
- ¼ teaspoon paprika
- Salt and freshly ground white pepper, to taste
- 2 egg whites
- ¾ cup panko breadcrumbs
- ½ cup unsweetened coconut, shredded
- 2 teaspoons lemon zest, grated finely
- 1 pound prawns, peeled and deveined

Preparation:

1. In a shallow dish, place the flour, paprika, salt and white pepper and mix well.
2. In a second shallow dish, add the egg whites and beat lightly.
3. In a third shallow dish, place the breadcrumbs, coconut and lemon zest and mix well.
4. Coat the prawns with flour mixture, then dip into egg whites and finally coat with the coconut mixture.
5. Place the prawns in the greased sheet pan.
6. Press "Power Button" of Ninja Foodi Digital Air Fry Oven and turn the dial to select "Air Bake" mode.
7. Press "Time Button" and again turn the dial to set the cooking time to 12 minutes.
8. Now push "Temp Button" and rotate the dial to set the temperature at 400 degrees F.
9. Press "Start/Pause" button to start.
10. When the unit beeps to show that it is preheated, open the lid and insert the sheet pan in the oven.
11. Flip the prawns once halfway through.
12. When cooking time is complete, open the lid and transfer the prawns onto a platter.
13. Serve hot.

Serving Suggestions: Sweet chili sauce will accompany these prawns nicely.

Variation Tip: You may use regular breadcrumbs instead of panko.

Nutritional Information per Serving:

Calories: 310|**Fat:** 6.9g|**Sat Fat:** 4.1g|**Carbohydrates:** 18.7g|**Fiber:** 1.5g|**Sugar:** 0.9g|**Protein:** 3.2g

Buffalo Chicken Wings

Preparation Time: 15 minutes
Cooking Time: 16 minutes
Servings: 5

Ingredients:

- 2 pounds frozen chicken wings, drums and flats separated
- 2 tablespoons olive oil
- 2-4 tablespoons Buffalo sauce
- ½ teaspoon red pepper flakes, crushed
- Salt, to taste

Preparation:

1. Coat the chicken wings with oil evenly.
2. Press "Power Button" of Ninja Foodi Digital Air Fry Oven and turn the dial to select "Air Fry" mode.
3. Press "Time Button" and again turn the dial to set the cooking time to 16 minutes.
4. Now push "Temp Button" and rotate the dial to set the temperature at 390 degrees F.
5. Press "Start/Pause" button to start.
6. When the unit beeps to show that it is preheated, open the lid.
7. Arrange the chicken wings into the air fry basket and insert in the oven.
8. After 7 minutes, flip the wings.
9. Meanwhile, in a large bowl, add the Buffalo sauce, red pepper flakes and salt and mix well.
10. When cooking time is complete, open the lid.
11. Transfer the wings into the bowl of Buffalo sauce and toss to coat well.
12. Serve immediately.

Serving Suggestions: Serving with blue cheese dip enhances the taste of these wings.

Variation Tip: To avoid spiciness, add a little sweetener in the sauce mixture.

Nutritional Information per Serving:

Calories: 394|**Fat:** 19.1g|**Sat Fat:** 4.5g|**Carbohydrates:** 0.2g|**Fiber:** 0.1g|**Sugar:** 0.1g|**Protein:** 52.5g

Spicy Chickpeas

Preparation Time: 5 minutes
Cooking Time: 10 minutes
Servings: 4

Ingredients:

- 1 (15-ounce) can chickpeas, rinsed and drained
- 1 tablespoon olive oil
- ½ teaspoon cayenne pepper
- ½ teaspoon smoked paprika
- ½ teaspoon ground cumin
- 1/8 teaspoon ground cinnamon
- Salt, to taste

Preparation:

1. In a bowl, add all the ingredients and toss to coat well.
2. Press "Power Button" of Ninja Foodi Digital Air Fry Oven and turn the dial to select "Air Fry" mode.
3. Press "Time Button" and again turn the dial to set the cooking time to 10 minutes.
4. Now push "Temp Button" and rotate the dial to set the temperature at 390 degrees F.
5. Press "Start/Pause" button to start.
6. When the unit beeps to show that it is preheated, open the lid.
7. Arrange the chickpeas into the air fry basket and insert in the oven.
8. When cooking time is complete, open the lid and transfer the chickpeas into a bowl.
9. Serve warm.

Serving Suggestions: These roasted chickpeas can also be used as a topping of potato soup.

Variation Tip: You can adjust the ratio of spices according to your taste.

Nutritional Information per Serving:

Calories: 146|**Fat:** 4.5g|**Sat Fat:** 0.5g|**Carbohydrates:** 18.8g|**Fiber:** 4.6g|**Sugar:** 0.1g|**Protein:** 6.3g

Cheese Pastries

Preparation Time: 15 minutes
Cooking Time: 10 minutes
Servings: 6

Ingredients:

- 1 egg yolk
- 4 ounces feta cheese, crumbled
- 1 scallion, finely chopped
- 2 tablespoons fresh parsley, finely chopped
- Salt and freshly ground black pepper, to taste
- 2 frozen phyllo pastry sheets, thawed
- 2 tablespoons olive oil

Preparation:

1. In a large bowl, add the egg yolk, and beat well.
2. Add the feta cheese, scallion, parsley, salt, and black pepper and mix well.
3. Cut each pastry sheet in three strips.
4. Add about 1 teaspoon of feta mixture on the underside of a strip.
5. Fold the tip of the pastry sheet over the filling in a zigzag manner to form a triangle.
6. Repeat with the remaining strips and fillings.
7. Coat each pastry with oil evenly.
8. Press "Power Button" of Ninja Foodi Digital Air Fry Oven and turn the dial to select "Air Fry" mode.
9. Press "Time Button" and again turn the dial to set the cooking time to 3 minutes.
10. Now push "Temp Button" and rotate the dial to set the temperature at 390 degrees F.
11. Press "Start/Pause" button to start.
12. When the unit beeps to show that it is preheated, open the lid.
13. Arrange the pastries in the air fry basket and insert in the oven.
14. After 3 minutes, set the temperature at 390 degrees F for 2 minutes.
15. When cooking time is complete, open the lid and transfer the pastries onto a platter.
16. Serve warm.

Serving Suggestions: Serve these pastries with marinara sauce.

Variation Tip: Feta cheese can be replaced with ricotta cheese too.

Nutritional Information per Serving:

Calories: 128|**Fat:** 10g|**Sat Fat:** 3.9g|**Carbohydrates:** 6g|**Fiber:** 0.3g|**Sugar:** 0.9g|**Protein:** 3.9g

Mozzarella Sticks

Preparation Time: 15 minutes
Cooking Time: 12 minutes
Servings: 3

Ingredients:

- ¼ cup white flour
- 2 eggs
- 3 tablespoons nonfat milk
- 1 cup plain breadcrumbs
- 1 pound Mozzarella cheese block, cut into 3x½-inch sticks

Preparation:

1. In a shallow dish, place the flour.
2. In a second shallow dish, add the eggs and milk and beat slightly.
3. In a third shallow dish, place the breadcrumbs.
4. Coat the Mozzarella sticks with flour, then dip into the egg mixture and finally, coat evenly with the breadcrumbs.
5. Press "Power Button" of Ninja Foodi Digital Air Fry Oven and turn the dial to select "Air Fry" mode.
6. Press "Time Button" and again turn the dial to set the cooking time to 12 minutes.
7. Now push "Temp Button" and rotate the dial to set the temperature at 400 degrees F.
8. Press "Start/Pause" button to start.
9. When the unit beeps to show that it is preheated, open the lid.
10. Arrange the mozzarella sticks in the air fry basket and insert in the oven.
11. When cooking time is complete, open the lid and transfer the mozzarella sticks onto a platter.
12. Serve warm

Serving Suggestions: Serve these mozzarella sticks with marinara sauce or ranch dressing.

Variation Tip: Cut the mozzarella into uniform sized sticks.

Nutritional Information per Serving:

Calories: 254|**Fat:** 6.6g|**Sat Fat:** 2.4g|**Carbohydrates:** 35.2g|**Fiber:** 1.4g|**Sugar:** 3.2g|**Protein:** 12.8g

Jalapeño Poppers

Preparation Time: 15 minutes
Cooking Time: 13 minutes
Servings: 6

Ingredients:

- 12 large jalapeño peppers
- 8 ounces cream cheese, softened
- ¼ cup scallion, chopped
- ¼ cup fresh cilantro, chopped
- ¼ teaspoon onion powder
- ¼ teaspoon garlic powder
- Salt, to taste
- 1/3 cup sharp cheddar cheese, grated

Preparation:

1. Carefully cut off one-third of each pepper lengthwise and then scoop out the seeds and membranes.
2. In a bowl, mix together the cream cheese, scallion, cilantro, spices and salt.
3. Stuff each pepper with the cream cheese mixture and top with cheese.
4. Arrange the jalapeño peppers onto the greased sheet pan.
5. Press "Power Button" of Ninja Foodi Digital Air Fry Oven and turn the dial to select "Air Fry" mode.
6. Press "Time Button" and again turn the dial to set the cooking time to 13 minutes.
7. Now push "Temp Button" and rotate the dial to set the temperature at 400 degrees F.
8. Press "Start/Pause" button to start.
9. When the unit beeps to show that it is preheated, open the lid and insert the sheet pan in the oven.
10. When cooking time is complete, open the lid and transfer the jalapeño poppers onto a platter.
11. Serve immediately.

Serving Suggestions: NO

Variation Tip: NO

Nutritional Information per Serving:

Calories: 171|**Fat:** 15.7g|**Sat Fat:** 9.7g|**Carbohydrates:** 3.7g|**Fiber:** 1.3g|**Sugar:** 1.2g|**Protein:** 4.9g

Cheddar Biscuits

Preparation Time: 15 minutes
Cooking Time: 10 minutes
Servings: 8

Ingredients:

- 1/3 cup unbleached all-purpose flour
- 1/8 teaspoon cayenne pepper
- 1/8 teaspoon smoked paprika
- Pinch of garlic powder
- Salt and freshly ground black pepper, to taste
- ½ cup sharp cheddar cheese, shredded
- 2 tablespoons butter, softened
- Nonstick cooking spray

Preparation:

1. In a food processor, add the flour, spices, salt and black pepper and pulse until well combined.
2. Add the cheese and butter and pulse until a smooth dough forms.
3. Place the dough onto a lightly floured surface.
4. Make 16 small equal-sized balls from the dough and press each slightly.
5. Press "Power Button" of Ninja Foodi Digital Air Fry Oven and turn the dial to select "Air Bake" mode.
6. Press "Time Button" and again turn the dial to set the cooking time to 10 minutes.
7. Now push "Temp Button" and rotate the dial to set the temperature at 330 degrees F.
8. Press "Start/Pause" button to start.
9. When the unit beeps to show that it is preheated, open the lid and grease the air fry basket.
10. Arrange the biscuits into the prepared air fry basket and insert in the oven.
11. When cooking time is complete, open the lid and place the basket onto a wire rack for about 10 minutes.
12. Carefully invert the biscuits onto the wire rack to cool completely before serving.

Serving Suggestions: Serve these cheddar biscuits with the drizzling of garlic butter.

Variation Tip: For flaky layers, use cold butter.

Nutritional Information per Serving:

Calories: 73|**Fat:** 5.3g|**Sat Fat:** 3.3g|**Carbohydrates:** 4.1g|**Fiber:** 0.2g|**Sugar:** 0.1g|**Protein:** 2.3g

French Fries

Preparation Time: 15 minutes
Cooking Time: 30 minutes
Servings: 4

Ingredients:

- 1 pound potatoes, peeled and cut into strips
- 3 tablespoons olive oil
- ½ teaspoon onion powder
- ½ teaspoon garlic powder
- 1 teaspoon paprika

Preparation:

1. In a large bowl of water, soak the potato strips for about 1 hour.
2. Drain the potato strips well and pat them dry with paper towels.
3. In a large bowl, add the potato strips and the remaining ingredients and toss to coat well.
4. Press "Power Button" of Ninja Foodi Digital Air Fry Oven and turn the dial to select "Air Fry" mode.
5. Press "Time Button" and again turn the dial to set the cooking time to 30 minutes.
6. Now push "Temp Button" and rotate the dial to set the temperature at 375 degrees F.
7. Press "Start/Pause" button to start.
8. When the unit beeps to show that it is preheated, open the lid.
9. Arrange the potato fries into the air fry basket and insert in the oven.
10. When cooking time is complete, open the lid and transfer the fries onto a platter.
11. Serve warm.

Serving Suggestions: Serve these fries with ketchup.

Variation Tip: Choose starchy potatoes for fries.

Nutritional Information per Serving:

Calories: 172|**Fat:** 10.7g|**Sat Fat:** 1.5g|**Carbohydrates:** 18.6g|**Fiber:** 3g|**Sugar:** 1.6g|**Protein:** 2.1g

Poultry Recipes

Marinated Chicken Thighs

Preparation Time: 10 minutes
Cooking Time: 30 minutes
Servings: 4

Ingredients:

- 4 (6-ounce) bone-in, skin-on chicken thighs
- Salt and freshly ground black pepper, to taste
- ½ cup Italian salad dressing
- 1 teaspoon onion powder
- 1 teaspoon garlic powder

Preparation:

1. Season the chicken thighs with salt and black pepper evenly.
2. In a large bowl, add the chicken thighs and dressing and mix well.
3. Cover the bowl and refrigerate to marinate overnight.
4. Remove the chicken breast from the bowl and place onto a plate.
5. Sprinkle the chicken thighs with onion powder and garlic powder.
6. Press "Power Button" of Ninja Foodi Digital Air Fry Oven and turn the dial to select "Air Fry" mode.
7. Press "Time Button" and again turn the dial to set the cooking time to 30 minutes.
8. Now push "Temp Button" and rotate the dial to set the temperature at 360 degrees F.
9. Press "Start/Pause" button to start.
10. When the unit beeps to show that it is preheated, open the lid and grease the air fry basket.
11. Arrange the chicken thighs into the prepared basket and insert in the oven.
12. After 15 minutes of cooking, flip the chicken thighs once.
13. When cooking time is complete, open the lid and transfer the chicken thighs onto serving plates.
14. Serve hot.

Serving Suggestions: Enjoy with honey glazed baby carrots.

Variation Tip: Select the chicken thighs with a pinkish hue.

Nutritional Information per Serving:

Calories: 413|**Fat:** 21g|**Sat Fat:** 4.8g|**Carbohydrates:** 4.1g|**Fiber:** 0.1g|**Sugar:** 2.8g|**Protein:** 49.5g

Thyme Duck Breast

Preparation Time: 15 minutes
Cooking Time: 20 minutes
Servings: 2

Ingredients:

- 1 cup beer
- 1 tablespoon olive oil
- 1 teaspoon mustard
- 1 tablespoon fresh thyme, chopped
- Salt and freshly ground black pepper, to taste
- 1 (10½-ounce) duck breast

Preparation:

1. In a bowl, add the beer, oil, mustard, thyme, salt, and black pepper and mix well
2. Add the duck breast and coat with marinade generously.
3. Cover and refrigerate for about 4 hours.
4. Arrange the duck breast onto the greased sheet pan.
5. Press "Power Button" of Ninja Foodi Digital Air Fry Oven and turn the dial to select "Air Fry" mode.
6. Press "Time Button" and again turn the dial to set the cooking time to 20 minutes.
7. Now push "Temp Button" and rotate the dial to set the temperature at 390 degrees F.
8. Press "Start/Pause" button to start.
9. When the unit beeps to show that it is preheated, open the lid and insert the sheet pan in the oven.
10. Flip the duck breast once halfway through.
11. When cooking time is complete, open the lid and place the duck breast onto a cutting board for about 5 minutes before slicing.
12. With a sharp knife, cut the duck breast into desired size slices and serve.

Serving Suggestions: Duck meat goes really well with caramelized onions or balsamic reduction.

Variation Tip: Look for a plump, firm breast for best flav

Nutritional Information per or. **Serving:**

Calories: 315|**Fat:** 13.5g|**Sat Fat:** 1.1g|**Carbohydrates:** 5.7g|**Fiber:** 0.7g|**Sugar:** 0.1g|**Protein:** 33.8g

Glazed Turkey Breast

Preparation Time: 15 minutes| **Cooking Time:** 55 minutes| **Servings:** 10

Ingredients:

- 1 teaspoon dried thyme, crushed
- ½ teaspoon dried sage, crushed
- ½ teaspoon smoked paprika
- Salt and freshly ground black pepper, to taste
- 1 (5-pound) boneless turkey breast
- 2 teaspoons olive oil
- ¼ cup maple syrup
- 2 tablespoons Dijon mustard
- 1 tablespoon butter, softened

Preparation:

1. In a bowl, mix together the herbs, paprika, salt, and black pepper.
2. Coat the turkey breast with oil evenly.
3. Now, coat the outer side of turkey breast with herb mixture.
4. Press "Power Button" of Ninja Foodi Digital Air Fry Oven and turn the dial to select "Air Fry" mode.
5. Press "Time Button" and again turn the dial to set the cooking time to 55 minutes.
6. Now push "Temp Button" and rotate the dial to set the temperature at 350 degrees F.
7. Press "Start/Pause" button to start.
8. When the unit beeps to show that it is preheated, open the lid and grease the air fry basket.
9. Arrange the turkey breast into the prepared basket and insert in the oven.
10. While cooking, flip the turkey breast once after 25 minutes and then after 37 minutes.
11. Meanwhile, in a bowl, mix together the maple syrup, mustard, and butter.
12. After 50 minutes of cooking, press "Start/Pause" to pause cooking.
13. Remove the basket from Air Fryer and coat the turkey breast with glaze evenly.
14. Again, insert the basket in the oven and press "Start/Pause" to resume cooking.
15. When cooking time is complete, open the lid and place the turkey breast onto a cutting board for about 10 minutes before slicing.
16. With a sharp knife, cut the turkey breast into desired sized slices and serve.

Serving Suggestions: Green bean and goats cheese salad will be best for turkey meat.

Variation Tip: Place the turkey into the basket with the breast side down.

Nutritional Information per Serving:

Calories: 30w|**Fat:** 3.3g|**Sat Fat:** 0.9g|**Carbohydrates:** 5.6g|**Fiber:** 0.2g|**Sugar:** 4.7g|**Protein:** 26.2g

Breaded Chicken Breast

Preparation Time: 15 minutes
Cooking Time: 12 minutes
Servings: 6

Ingredients:

- 1 cup breadcrumbs
- ½ cup Parmesan cheese, grated
- ¼ cup fresh parsley, minced
- Salt and freshly ground black pepper, to taste
- 1½ pounds boneless, skinless chicken breasts
- 3 tablespoons olive oil
- Olive oil cooking spray

Preparation:

1. In a shallow dish, add the breadcrumbs, Parmesan cheese, parsley, salt and black pepper mix well.
2. Rub the chicken breasts with oil and then, coat with the breadcrumbs mixture evenly.
3. Arrange the chicken breasts onto the sheet pan and spray with cooking spray.
4. Press "Power Button" of Ninja Foodi Digital Air Fry Oven and turn the dial to select "Air Fry" mode.
5. Press "Time Button" and again turn the dial to set the cooking time to 12 minutes.
6. Now push "Temp Button" and rotate the dial to set the temperature at 350 degrees F.
7. Press "Start/Pause" button to start.
8. When the unit beeps to show that it is preheated, open the lid and insert the sheet pan in the oven.
9. Flip the chicken breasts once halfway through.
10. When cooking time is complete, open the lid and transfer the chicken breasts onto a platter.
11. Serve hot.

Serving Suggestions: Enjoy these chicken breasts with honey mustard sauce.

Variation Tip: Pat dry the chicken breasts thoroughly before breading.

Nutritional Information per Serving:

Calories: 371|**Fat:** 18g|**Sat Fat:** 4.3g|**Carbohydrates:** 13.1g|**Fiber:** 0.9g|**Sugar:** 1.1g|**Protein:** 38g

Garlicky Duck Legs

Preparation Time: 10 minutes| **Cooking Time:** 30 minutes
Servings: 2

Ingredients:

- 2 garlic cloves, minced
- 1 tablespoon fresh parsley, chopped
- 1 teaspoon five-spice powder
- Salt and freshly ground black pepper, to taste
- 2 duck legs

Preparation:

1. In a bowl, mix together the garlic, parsley, five-spice powder, salt and black pepper.
2. Rub the duck legs with garlic mixture generously.
3. Arrange the duck legs onto the greased sheet pan.
4. Press "Power Button" of Ninja Foodi Digital Air Fry Oven and turn the dial to select "Air Fry" mode.
5. Press "Time Button" and again turn the dial to set the cooking time to 30 minutes.
6. Now push "Temp Button" and rotate the dial to set the temperature at 340 degrees F.
7. Press "Start/Pause" button to start.
8. When the unit beeps to show that it is preheated, open the lid and insert the sheet pan in the oven.
9. Flip the duck legs once halfway through.
10. When cooking time is complete, open the lid and transfer the duck legs onto serving plates.
11. Serve hot.

Serving Suggestions: Serve these duck legs with cucmber salad.

Variation Tip: Never defrost the duck meat on the counter.

Nutritional Information per Serving:

Calories: 434|**Fat:** 14.4g|**Sat Fat:** 3.2g|**Carbohydrates:** 1.1g|**Fiber:** 0.1g|**Sugar:** 0.1g| **Protein:** 70.4g

Herbed Chicken Drumsticks

Preparation Time: 10 minutes
Cooking Time: 20 minutes
Servings: 2

Ingredients:

- 1 tablespoon olive oil
- ½ teaspoon dried thyme, crushed
- ½ teaspoon dried rosemary, crushed
- ½ teaspoon oregano, crushed
- Salt and freshly ground black pepper, to taste
- 2 (6-ounce) chicken drumsticks

Preparation:

1. In a large bowl, place the oil, herbs, salt and black pepper and mix well.
2. Add the chicken drumsticks and coat with the mixture generously.
3. Place the chicken drumsticks into the greased baking pan.
4. Press "Power Button" of Ninja Foodi Digital Air Fry Oven and turn the dial to select "Air Fry" mode.
5. Press "Time Button" and again turn the dial to set the cooking time to 20 minutes.
6. Now push "Temp Button" and rotate the dial to set the temperature at 375 degrees F.
7. Press "Start/Pause" button to start.
8. When the unit beeps to show that it is preheated, open the lid and insert the baking pan in the oven.
9. When cooking time is complete, open the lid and transfer the chicken drumsticks onto serving plates.
10. Serve hot.

Serving Suggestions: Any kind of dipping sauce will be great for these drumsticks.

Variation Tip: You can use fresh herbs instead of dried herbs.

Nutritional Information per Serving:

Calories: 350|**Fat:** 16.8g|**Sat Fat:** 3.6g|**Carbohydrates:** 0.6g|**Fiber:** 0.4g|**Sugar:** 0g|**Protein:** 46.9g

Lemony Turkey Legs

Preparation Time: 10 minutes
Cooking Time: 30 minutes
Servings: 2

Ingredients:

- 2 garlic cloves, minced
- 1 tablespoon fresh rosemary, minced
- 1 teaspoon fresh lemon zest, finely grated
- 2 tablespoons olive oil
- 1 tablespoon fresh lemon juice
- Salt and freshly ground black pepper, to taste
- 2 turkey legs

Preparation:

1. In a large bowl, mix together the garlic, rosemary, lime zest, oil, lime juice, salt, and black pepper.
2. Add the turkey legs and coat with marinade generously.
3. Refrigerate to marinate for about 6-8 hours.
4. Press "Power Button" of Ninja Foodi Digital Air Fry Oven and turn the dial to select "Air Fry" mode.
5. Press "Time Button" and again turn the dial to set the cooking time to 30 minutes.
6. Now push "Temp Button" and rotate the dial to set the temperature at 350 degrees F.
7. Press "Start/Pause" button to start.
8. When the unit beeps to show that it is preheated, open the lid and grease the air fry basket.
9. Arrange the turkey legs into the prepared basket and insert in the oven.
10. Flip the turkey legs once halfway through.
11. When cooking time is complete, open the lid and transfer the turkey legs onto serving plates.
12. Serve hot.

Serving Suggestions: Serve these turkey legs with honey macadamia stuffing.

Variation Tip: A fresh turkey meat should never be chilled below 26 degrees.

Nutritional Information per Serving:

Calories: 709|**Fat:** 32.7g|**Sat Fat:** 7.8g|**Carbohydrates:** 2.3g|**Fiber:** 0.8g|**Sugar:** 0.1g|**Protein:** 97.2g

Chicken Cordon Bleu

Preparation Time: 15 minutes | **Cooking Time:** 30 minutes| **Servings:** 2

Ingredients:

- 2 (6-ounce) boneless, skinless chicken breast halves, pounded into ¼-inch thickness
- 2 (¾-ounce) deli ham slices
- 2 Swiss cheese slices
- ½ cup all-purpose flour
- 1/8 teaspoon paprika
- Salt and freshly ground black pepper, to taste
- 1 large egg
- 2 tablespoons 2% milk
- ½ cup seasoned breadcrumbs
- 1 tablespoon olive oil
- 1 tablespoon butter, melted

Preparation:

1. Arrange the chicken breast halves onto a smooth surface.
2. Arrange 1 ham slice over each chicken breast half, followed by the cheese.
3. Roll up each chicken breast half and tuck in ends.
4. With toothpicks, secure the rolls.
5. In a shallow plate, mix together the flour, paprika, salt and black pepper.
6. In a shallow bowl, place the egg and milk and beat slightly.
7. In a second shallow plate, place the breadcrumbs.
8. Coat each chicken roll with flour mixture, then dip into the egg mixture and finally coat with breadcrumbs.
9. In a small skillet, heat the oil over medium heat and cook the chicken rolls for about 3-5 minutes or until browned from all sides.
10. Transfer the chicken rolls into the greased sheet pan.
11. Press "Power Button" of Ninja Foodi Digital Air Fry Oven and turn the dial to select "Air Bake" mode.
12. Press "Time Button" and again turn the dial to set the cooking time to 25 minutes.
13. Now push "Temp Button" and rotate the dial to set the temperature at 350 degrees F.
14. Press "Start/Pause" button to start.
15. When the unit beeps to show that it is preheated, open the lid and insert the sheet pan in the oven.
16. When cooking time is complete, open the lid and transfer the chicken rolls onto a platter.
17. Discard the toothpicks and drizzle the rolls with melted butter.
18. Serve immediately.

Serving Suggestions: Enjoy with Dijon sauce.

Variation Tip: Carefully roll the chicken breasts until the filling in the middle with the chicken wrapped completely around the outside.

Nutritional Information per Serving:

Calories: 672|**Fat:** 28g|**Sat Fat:** 9.3g |**Carbohydrates:** 45.9g|**Fiber:** 2.4g|**Sugar:** 3.4g| **Protein:** 56.2g

Spiced Chicken Thighs

Preparation Time: 15 minutes
Cooking Time: 20 minutes
Servings: 4

Ingredients:

- 1 teaspoon ground cumin
- 1 teaspoon garlic powder
- ½ teaspoon smoked paprika
- ½ teaspoon ground coriander
- Salt and ground black pepper, as required
- 4 (5-ounce) chicken thighs

Preparation:

1. In a large bowl, add the spices, salt and black pepper and mix well.
2. Coat the chicken thighs with oil and then rub with spice mixture.
3. Arrange the chicken thighs onto the sheet pan.
4. Press "Power Button" of Ninja Foodi Digital Air Fry Oven and turn the dial to select "Air Fry" mode.
5. Press "Time Button" and again turn the dial to set the cooking time to 20 minutes.
6. Now push "Temp Button" and rotate the dial to set the temperature at 400 degrees F.
7. Press "Start/Pause" button to start.
8. When the unit beeps to show that it is preheated, open the lid and insert the sheet pan in the oven.
9. Flip the chicken thighs once halfway through.
10. When cooking time is complete, open the lid and transfer the chicken thighs onto serving plates.
11. Serve hot.

Serving Suggestions: Serve with a fresh green salad.

Variation Tip: Adjust the ratio of spices according to your spice tolerance.

Nutritional Information per Serving:

Calories: 334|**Fat:** 17.7g|**Sat Fat:** 3.9g|**Carbohydrates:** 0.9g|**Fiber:** 0.2g|**Sugar:** 0.2g|**Protein:** 41.3g

Glazed Chicken Drumsticks

Preparation Time: 10 minutes
Cooking Time: 20 minutes
Servings: 4

Ingredients:

- ¼ cup Dijon mustard
- 1 tablespoon maple syrup
- 2 tablespoons olive oil
- 1 tablespoon fresh rosemary, minced
- Salt and freshly ground black pepper, to taste
- 4 (6-ounce) chicken drumsticks

Preparation:

1. Marinated the chicken drumsticks with all the above ingredients for overnight. Preheat Philips Air fryer at 160 degree. In a bowl, add all ingredients except the drumsticks and mix until well combined.
2. Add the drumsticks and coat with the mixture generously.
3. Cover the bowl and refrigerate to marinate overnight.
4. Place the chicken drumsticks into the greased baking pan.
5. Press "Power Button" of Ninja Foodi Digital Air Fry Oven and turn the dial to select "Air Fry" mode.
6. Press "Time Button" and again turn the dial to set the cooking time to 12 minutes.
7. Now push "Temp Button" and rotate the dial to set the temperature at 320 degrees F.
8. Press "Start/Pause" button to start.
9. When the unit beeps to show that it is preheated, open the lid and insert baking pan in the oven.
10. After 12 minutes, flip the drumsticks and set the temperature to 390 degrees F for 8 minutes.
11. When cooking time is complete, open the lid and transfer the chicken drumsticks onto serving plates.
12. Serve hot.

Serving Suggestions: NO

Variation Tip: You can increase the quantity of maple syrup according to your taste.

Nutritional Information per Serving:

Calories: 374|**Fat:** 17.5g|**Sat Fat:** 3.7g|**Carbohydrates:** 4.7g|**Fiber:** 0.9g|**Sugar:** 3.1g|**Protein:** 47.5g

Herbed Roasted Chicken

Preparation Time: 15 minutes
Cooking Time: 1 hour 10 minutes
Servings: 6

Ingredients:

- ¼ cup butter, softened
- 1 teaspoon dried rosemary, crushed
- 1 teaspoon dried basil, crushed
- 1 teaspoon dried oregano, crushed
- 1 teaspoon dried thyme, crushed
- 1 tablespoon garlic powder
- 1 tablespoon paprika
- 1 tablespoon ground cumin
- Salt and freshly ground black pepper, to taste
- 1 (3-pound) whole chicken, neck and giblets removed

Preparation:

1. In a bowl, add the butter, herbs, spices and salt and mix well.
2. Rub the chicken with spice mixture generously.
3. With kitchen twine, tie off wings and legs.
4. Arrange the chicken onto the greased sheet pan.
5. Press "Power Button" of Ninja Foodi Digital Air Fry Oven and turn the dial to select "Air Bake" mode.
6. Press "Time Button" and again turn the dial to set the cooking time to 70 minutes.
7. Now push "Temp Button" and rotate the dial to set the temperature at 380 degrees F.
8. Press "Start/Pause" button to start.
9. When the unit beeps to show that it is preheated, open the lid and insert the sheet pan in oven.
10. When cooking time is complete, open the lid and place the chicken onto a platter for about 10-15 minutes before carving.
11. With a sharp knife, cut the chicken into desired sized pieces and serve.

Serving Suggestions: Roasted vegetables will accompany this roasted chicken nicely.

Variation Tip: Rub the chicken with your hands for even coating.

Nutritional Information per Serving:

Calories: 434|**Fat:** 15g|**Sat Fat:** 6.9g|**Carbohydrates:** 2.5g|**Fiber:** 0.9g|**Sugar:** 0.5g|**Protein:** 66.4g

Herbed Turkey Breast

Preparation Time: 15 minutes
Cooking Time: 40 minutes
Servings: 6

Ingredients:

- ¼ cup unsalted butter, softened
- 2 tablespoons fresh rosemary, chopped
- 2 tablespoon fresh thyme, chopped
- 2 tablespoons fresh sage, chopped
- 2 tablespoons fresh parsley, chopped
- Salt and freshly ground black pepper, to taste
- 1 (4-pound) bone-in, skin-on turkey breast
- 2 tablespoons olive oil

Preparation:

1. In a bowl, add the butter, herbs, salt and black pepper and mix well.
2. Rub the herb mixture under skin evenly.
3. Coat the outside of turkey breast with oil.
4. Place the turkey breast into the greased baking pan.
5. Press "Power Button" of Ninja Foodi Digital Air Fry Oven and turn the dial to select "Air Bake" mode.
6. Press "Time Button" and again turn the dial to set the cooking time to 40 minutes.
7. Now push "Temp Button" and rotate the dial to set the temperature at 350 degrees F.
8. Press "Start/Pause" button to start.
9. When the unit beeps to show that it is preheated, open the lid and insert baking pan in the oven.
10. When cooking time is complete, open the lid and place the turkey breast onto a platter for about 5-10 minutes before slicing.
11. With a sharp knife, cut the turkey breast into desired sized slices and serve.

Serving Suggestions: Roasted potatoes will accompany this turkey breast nicely.

Variation Tip: Use unsalted butter.

Nutritional Information per Serving:

Calories: 333|**Fat:** 37g|**Sat Fat:** 12.4g|**Carbohydrates:** 1.8g|**Fiber:** 1.1g|**Sugar:** 0.1g|**Protein:** 65.1g

Roasted Cornish Game Hen

Preparation Time: 20 minutes
Cooking Time: 16 minutes
Servings: 4

Ingredients:

- ¼ cup olive oil
- 1 teaspoon fresh rosemary, chopped
- 1 teaspoon fresh thyme, chopped
- 1 teaspoon fresh lemon zest, finely grated
- ¼ teaspoon sugar
- ¼ teaspoon red pepper flakes, crushed
- Salt and freshly ground black pepper, to taste
- 2 pounds Cornish game hen, backbone removed and halved

Preparation:

1. In a bowl, mix together oil, herbs, lemon zest, sugar, and spices.
2. Add the hen portions and coat with the marinade generously.
3. Cover and refrigerate for about 24 hours.
4. In a strainer, place the hen portions and set aside to drain any liquid.
5. Press "Power Button" of Ninja Foodi Digital Air Fry Oven and turn the dial to select "Air Fry" mode.
6. Press "Time Button" and again turn the dial to set the cooking time to 16 minutes.
7. Now push "Temp Button" and rotate the dial to set the temperature at 390 degrees F.
8. Press "Start/Pause" button to start.
9. When the unit beeps to show that it is preheated, open the lid and grease the air fry basket.
10. Arrange the hen portions into the prepared basket and insert in the oven.
11. When cooking time is complete, open the lid and transfer the hen portions onto a platter.
12. Cut each portion in half and serve.

Serving Suggestions: Serve with dinner rolls.

Variation Tip: Place the hens in the basket, breast side up.

Nutritional Information per Serving:

Calories: 557|**Fat:** 45.1g|**Sat Fat:** 1.8g|**Carbohydrates:** 0.8g|**Fiber:** 0.3g|**Sugar:** 0.3g|**Protein:** 38.5g

Spicy Chicken Legs

Preparation Time: 10 minutes
Cooking Time: 25 minutes
Servings: 6

Ingredients:

- 2½ pounds chicken legs
- 2 tablespoons olive oil
- 1 teaspoon smoked paprika
- 1 teaspoon garlic powder
- ½ teaspoon ground cumin
- Salt and freshly ground black pepper, to taste

Preparation:

1. In a large bowl, add all the ingredients and mix well.
2. Arrange the chicken legs onto a sheet pan.
3. Press "Power Button" of Ninja Foodi Digital Air Fry Oven and turn the dial to select "Air Fry" mode.
4. Press "Time Button" and again turn the dial to set the cooking time to 25 minutes.
5. Now push "Temp Button" and rotate the dial to set the temperature at 400 degrees F.
6. Press "Start/Pause" button to start.
7. When the unit beeps to show that it is preheated, open the lid and insert the sheet pan in the oven.
8. When cooking time is complete, open the lid and transfer the chicken legs onto serving plates.
9. Serve hot.

Serving Suggestions: Serve with cheesy baked asparagus.

Variation Tip: Don't accept any chicken legs that are soft and discolored.

Nutritional Information per Serving:

Calories: 402|**Fat:** 18.8g|**Sat Fat:** 4.5g|**Carbohydrates:** 0.6g|**Fiber:** 0.2g|**Sugar:** 0.2g|**Protein:** 54.8g

Rosemary Chicken Thighs

Preparation Time: 10 minutes
Cooking Time: 20 minutes
Servings: 2

Ingredients:

- 2 (4-ounces) skinless, boneless chicken thighs
- 1 teaspoon fresh rosemary, minced
- Salt and freshly ground black pepper, to taste
- 2 tablespoons butter, melted

Preparation:

1. Rub the chicken thighs with salt and black pepper evenly and then brush with melted butter.
2. Place the chicken thighs into the greased baking pan.
3. Press "Power Button" of Ninja Foodi Digital Air Fry Oven and turn the dial to select "Air Bake" mode.
4. Press "Time Button" and again turn the dial to set the cooking time to 20 minutes.
5. Now push "Temp Button" and rotate the dial to set the temperature at 450 degrees F.
6. Press "Start/Pause" button to start.
7. When the unit beeps to show that it is preheated, open the lid and insert baking pan in the oven.
8. When cooking time is complete, open the lid and transfer the chicken thighs onto serving plates.
9. Serve hot.

Serving Suggestions: Mashed potatoes will go great with these cooked chicken thighs.

Variation Tip: Olive oil can replace butter in this recipe.

Nutritional Information per Serving:

Calories: 246|**Fat:** 15.7g|**Sat Fat:** 8.9g|**Carbohydrates:** 0.4g|**Fiber:** 0.3g|**Sugar:** 0g|**Protein:** 25.5g

Bacon-Wrapped Chicken Breasts

Preparation Time: 15 minutes| **Cooking Time:** 23 minutes
Servings: 4

Ingredients:

- 1 tablespoon palm sugar
- 6-7 Fresh basil leaves
- 2 tablespoons fish sauce
- 2 tablespoons water
- 2 (8-ounces) chicken breasts, cut each breast in half horizontally
- Salt and freshly ground black pepper, to taste
- 12 bacon strips
- 1½ teaspoon honey

Preparation:

1. In a small heavy-bottomed pan, add palm sugar over medium-low heat and cook for about 2-3 minutes or until caramelized, stirring continuously.
2. Add the basil, fish sauce and water and stir to combine.
3. Remove from heat and transfer the sugar mixture into a large bowl.
4. Sprinkle each chicken breast with salt and black pepper.
5. Add the chicken pieces in the sugar mixture and coat generously.
6. Refrigerate to marinate for about 4-6 hours.
7. Wrap each chicken piece with 3 bacon strips.
8. Coat each piece with honey slightly.
9. Press "Power Button" of Ninja Foodi Digital Air Fry Oven and turn the dial to select "Air Fry" mode.
10. Press "Time Button" and again turn the dial to set the cooking time to 20 minutes.
11. Now push "Temp Button" and rotate the dial to set the temperature at 365 degrees F.
12. Press "Start/Pause" button to start.
13. When the unit beeps to show that it is preheated, open the lid and grease the air fry basket.
14. Arrange the chicken breasts into the prepared basket and insert in the oven.
15. Flip the chicken breasts once halfway through.
16. When cooking time is complete, open the lid and transfer the chicken breasts onto serving plates.
17. Serve hot.

Serving Suggestions: Serve with balsamic-glazed green beans.

Variation Tip: Use thick-cut bacon strips.

Nutritional Information per Serving:

Calories: 709|**Fat:** 44.8g|**Sat Fat:** 14.3g|**Carbohydrates:** 6.8g|**Fiber:** 0g|**Sugar:** 4.7g| **Protein:** 65.6g

Beef, Pork & Lamb Recipes

Glazed Lamb Meatballs

Preparation Time: 15 minutes| **Cooking Time:** 30 minutes| **Servings:** 8

Ingredients:

For Meatballs:

- 2 pounds lean ground lamb
- 2/3 cup quick-cooking oats
- ½ cup Ritz crackers, crushed
- 1 (5-ounce) can evaporated milk
- 2 large eggs, beaten lightly
- 1 teaspoon maple syrup
- 1 tablespoon dried onion, minced
- Salt and freshly ground black pepper, to taste

For Sauce:

- 1/3 cup orange marmalade
- 1/3 cup maple syrup
- 1/3 cup sugar
- 2 tablespoons cornstarch
- 2 tablespoons soy sauce
- 1-2 tablespoons Sriracha
- 1 tablespoon Worcestershire sauce

Preparation:

1. For meatballs: in a large bowl, add all the ingredients and mix until well combined.
2. Make 1½-inch balls from the mixture.
3. Arrange half of the meatballs onto the greased sheet pan in a single layer.
4. Press "Power Button" of Ninja Foodi Digital Air Fry Oven and turn the dial to select "Air Fry" mode.
5. Press "Time Button" and again turn the dial to set the cooking time to 15 minutes.
6. Now push "Temp Button" and rotate the dial to set the temperature at 380 degrees F.
7. Press "Start/Pause" button to start.
8. When the unit beeps to show that it is preheated, open the lid and insert the sheet pan in the oven.
9. Flip the meatballs once halfway through.
10. When cooking time is complete, open the lid and transfer the meatballs into a bowl.
11. Repeat with the remaining meatballs.
12. Meanwhile, for sauce: in a small pan, add all the ingredients over medium heat and cook until thickened, stirring continuously.
13. Serve the meatballs with the topping of sauce.

Serving Suggestions: Mashed buttery potatoes make a classic pairing with meatballs.

Variation Tip: You can adjust the ratio of sweetener according to your taste.

Nutritional Information per Serving:

Calories: 413|**Fat:** 11.9g|**Sat Fat:** 4.3g|**Carbohydrates:** 39.5g|**Fiber:** 1g|**Sugar:** 28.2g|**Protein:** 36.2g

Spiced Flank Steak

Preparation Time: 10 minutes
Cooking Time: 12 minutes
Servings: 6

Ingredients:

- 2 tablespoons balsamic vinegar
- 2 tablespoons olive oil
- 3 garlic cloves, minced
- 1 teaspoon red chili powder
- 1 teaspoon ground cumin
- 1 teaspoon onion powder
- Salt and freshly ground black pepper, to taste
- 1 (2-pound) flank steak

Preparation:

1. In a large bowl, mix together the vinegar, spices, salt and black pepper.
2. Add the steak and coat with mixture generously.
3. Cover the bowl and place in the refrigerator for at least 1 hour.
4. Remove the steak from bowl and place onto the greased sheet pan.
5. Press "Power Button" of Ninja Foodi Digital Air Fry Oven and turn the dial to select the "Air Broil" mode.
6. Press "Time Button" and again turn the dial to set the cooking time to 12 minutes.
7. Press "Start/Pause" button to start.
8. When the unit beeps to show that it is preheated, open the lid and insert the sheet pan in the oven.
9. Flip the steak once halfway through.
10. When cooking time is complete, open the lid and place the steak onto a cutting board.
11. With a sharp knife, cut the steak into desired sized slices and serve.

Serving Suggestions: Enjoy this steak with a drizzling of fresh lemon juice.

Variation Tip: choose the steak that is as uniform in thickness.

Nutritional Information per Serving:

Calories: 341|**Fat:** 17.4g|**Sat Fat:** 5.9g|**Carbohydrates:** 1.3g|**Fiber:** 0.2g|**Sugar:** 0.2g|**Protein:** 42.3g

Pork Meatloaf

Preparation Time: 15 minutes| **Cooking Time:** 1 hour 5 minutes| **Servings:** 8

Ingredients:

For Meatloaf:

- 2 pounds lean ground pork
- 1 cup quick-cooking oats
- ½ cup carrot, peeled and shredded
- 1 medium onion, chopped
- ½ cup fat-free milk
- ¼ of egg, beaten
- 2 tablespoons ketchup
- 1 teaspoon garlic powder
- ¼ teaspoon ground black pepper

For Topping:

- ¼ cup ketchup
- ¼ cup quick-cooking oats

Preparation:

1. For meatloaf: in a bowl, add all the ingredients and mix until well combined.
2. For topping: in another bowl, add all the ingredients and mix until well combined.
3. Transfer the mixture into a greased loaf pan and top with the topping mixture.
4. Press "Power Button" of Ninja Foodi Digital Air Fry Oven and turn the dial to select "Air Bake" mode.
5. Press "Time Button" and again turn the dial to set the cooking time to 65 minutes.
6. Now push "Temp Button" and rotate the dial to set the temperature at 350 degrees F.
7. Press "Start/Pause" button to start.
8. When the unit beeps to show that it is preheated, open the lid.
9. Arrange the loaf pan over the wire rack and insert in the oven.
10. When cooking time is complete, open the lid and place the loaf pan onto a wire rack for about 10 minutes.
11. Carefully invert the loaf onto the wire rack.
12. Cut into desired sized slices and serve.

Serving Suggestions: Baked cauliflower will nicely accompany this meatloaf.

Variation Tip: Add in a sprinkling of Italian seasoning in meatloaf.

Nutritional Information per Serving:

Calories: 239|**Fat:** 9.1g|**Sat Fat:** 2.7g|**Carbohydrates:** 14.5g|**Fiber:** 1.8g|**Sugar:** 4.5g|**Protein:** 25.1g

Glazed Pork Tenderloin

Preparation Time: 10 minutes
Cooking Time: 20 minutes
Servings: 3

Ingredients:

- 2 tablespoons Sriracha
- 2 tablespoons maple syrup
- ¼ teaspoon red pepper flakes, crushed
- Salt, to taste
- 1 pound pork tenderloin

Preparation:

1. In a small bowl, add the Sriracha, maple syrup, red pepper flakes and salt and mix well.
2. Brush the pork tenderloin with mixture evenly.
3. Press "Power Button" of Ninja Foodi Digital Air Fry Oven and turn the dial to select "Air Fry" mode.
4. Press "Time Button" and again turn the dial to set the cooking time to 20 minutes.
5. Now push "Temp Button" and rotate the dial to set the temperature at 350 degrees F.
6. Press "Start/Pause" button to start.
7. When the unit beeps to show that it is preheated, open the lid and grease air fry basket.
8. Arrange the pork tenderloin into the air fry basket and insert in the oven.
9. When cooking time is complete, open the lid and place the pork tenderloin onto a platter for about 10 minutes before slicing.
10. With a sharp knife, cut the roast into desired sized slices and serve.

Serving Suggestions: Fig and arugula salad will brighten the taste of tenderloin.

Variation Tip: The addition of dried herbs will add a delish touch in pork tenderloin.

Nutritional Information per Serving:

Calories: 261|**Fat:** 5.4g|**Sat Fat:** 1.8g|**Carbohydrates:** 11g|**Fiber:** 0g|**Sugar:** 8g|**Protein:** 39.6g

Buttered Leg of Lamb

Preparation Time: 15 minutes
Cooking Time: 1¼ hours
Servings: 8

Ingredients:

- 1 (2¼-pound) boneless leg of lamb
- 3 tablespoons butter, melted
- Salt and freshly ground black pepper, to taste
- 4 fresh rosemary sprigs

Preparation:

1. Rub the leg of lamb with butter and sprinkle with salt and black pepper.
2. Wrap the leg of lamb with rosemary sprigs.
3. Press "Power Button" of Ninja Foodi Digital Air Fry Oven and turn the dial to select "Air Fry" mode.
4. Press "Time Button" and again turn the dial to set the cooking time to 75 minutes.
5. Now push "Temp Button" and rotate the dial to set the temperature at 300 degrees F.
6. Press "Start/Pause" button to start.
7. When the unit beeps to show that it is preheated, open the lid and grease air fry basket.
8. Arrange the leg of lamb into the air fry basket and insert in the oven.
9. When cooking time is complete, open the lid and place the leg of lamb onto a cutting board for about 10 minutes before slicing.
10. Cut into desired sized pieces and serve.

Serving Suggestions: Dijon mustard glazed carrots will be great if served with le

Variation Tip: You can add spices of your choice for seasoning of the leg of lamb.

Nutritional Information per Serving:

Calories: 278|**Fat:** 13.8g|**Sat Fat:** 6.1g|**Carbohydrates:** 0.5g|**Fiber:** 0.4g|**Sugar:** 0g|**Protein:** 35.9g

Herbed Pork Chops

Preparation Time: 10 minutes
Cooking Time: 12 minutes
Servings: 3

Ingredients:

- 2 garlic cloves, minced
- ½ tablespoons fresh cilantro, chopped
- ½ tablespoons fresh rosemary, chopped
- ½ tablespoons fresh parsley, chopped
- 2 tablespoons olive oil
- ¾ tablespoons Dijon mustard
- 1 tablespoon ground coriander
- 1 teaspoon sugar
- Salt, to taste
- 3 (6-ounce) (1-inch thick) pork chops

Preparation:

1. In a bowl, mix together the garlic, herbs, oil, mustard, coriander, sugar, and salt.
2. Add the pork chops and coat with marinade generously.
3. Cover the bowl and refrigerate for about 2-3 hours.
4. Remove chops from the refrigerator and set aside at room temperature for about 30 minutes.
5. Press "Power Button" of Ninja Foodi Digital Air Fry Oven and turn the dial to select "Air Fry" mode.
6. Press "Time Button" and again turn the dial to set the cooking time to 12 minutes.
7. Now push "Temp Button" and rotate the dial to set the temperature at 390 degrees F.
8. Press "Start/Pause" button to start.
9. When the unit beeps to show that it is preheated, open the lid and grease the air fry basket.
10. Arrange chops into the prepared Air Fryer basket in a single layer and insert in the oven.
11. When cooking time is complete, open the lid and transfer the chops onto plates.
12. Serve hot.

Serving Suggestions: Serve thee chops with curried potato salad.

Variation Tip: Bring the pork chops to room temperature before cooking.

Nutritional Information per Serving:

Calories: 341|**Fat:** 25.5g|**Sat Fat:** 6.8g|**Carbohydrates:** 2.9g|**Fiber:** 0.4g|**Sugar:** 1.4g|**Protein:** 32.3g

Glazed Lamb Chops

Preparation Time: 10 minutes
Cooking Time: 15 minutes
Servings: 4

Ingredients:

- 1 tablespoon Dijon mustard
- ½ tablespoon fresh lime juice
- 1 teaspoon honey
- ½ teaspoon olive oil
- Salt and freshly ground black pepper, to taste
- 4 (4-ounce) lamb loin chops

Preparation:

1. In a black pepper large bowl, mix together the mustard, lemon juice, oil, honey, salt, and black pepper.
2. Add the chops and coat with the mixture generously.
3. Place the chops onto the greased sheet pan.
4. Press "Power Button" of Ninja Foodi Digital Air Fry Oven and turn the dial to select "Air Bake" mode.
5. Press "Time Button" and again turn the dial to set the cooking time to 15 minutes.
6. Now push "Temp Button" and rotate the dial to set the temperature at 390 degrees F.
7. Press "Start/Pause" button to start.
8. When the unit beeps to show that it is preheated, open the lid and insert the sheet pan in the oven.
9. Flip the chops once halfway through.
10. When cooking time is complete, open the lid and transfer the chops onto serving plates.
11. Serve hot.

Serving Suggestions: Serve the chops with mashed potatoes or polenta.

Variation Tip: Remember to pat dry the chops before seasoning.

Nutritional Information per Serving:

Calories: 224|**Fat:** 9.1g|**Sat Fat:** 3.1g|**Carbohydrates:** 1.7g|**Fiber:** 0.1g|**Sugar:** 1.5g|**Protein:** 32g

Stuffed Pork Roll

Preparation Time: 15 minutes
Cooking Time: 20 minutes
Servings: 4

Ingredients:

- 1 scallion, chopped
- ¼ cup sun-dried tomatoes, chopped finely
- 2 tablespoons fresh parsley, chopped
- Salt and freshly ground black pepper, to taste
- 4 (6-ounce) pork cutlets, pounded slightly
- 2 teaspoons paprika
- ½ tablespoons olive oil

Preparation:

1. In a bowl, mix together the scallion, tomatoes, parsley, salt, and black pepper.
2. Spread the tomato mixture over each pork cutlet.
3. Roll each cutlet and secure with cocktail sticks.
4. Rub the outer part of rolls with paprika, salt and black pepper.
5. Coat the rolls with oil evenly.
6. Press "Power Button" of Ninja Foodi Digital Air Fry Oven and turn the dial to select "Air Fry" mode.
7. Press "Time Button" and again turn the dial to set the cooking time to 15 minutes.
8. Now push "Temp Button" and rotate the dial to set the temperature at 390 degrees F.
9. Press "Start/Pause" button to start.
10. When the unit beeps to show that it is preheated, open the lid and grease air fry basket.
11. Arrange pork rolls into the prepared air fry basket in a single layer and insert in the oven.
12. When cooking time is complete, open the lid and transfer the pork rolls onto serving plates.
13. Serve hot.

Serving Suggestions: Serve these pork rolls with creamed spinach.

Variation Tip: Drain the sun-dried tomatoes completely before using them.

Nutritional Information per Serving:

Calories: 244|**Fat:** 14.5g|**Sat Fat:** 2.7g|**Carbohydrates:** 20.1g|**Fiber:** 2.6g|**Sugar:** 1.7g|**Protein:** 8.2g

Almonds Crusted Rack of Lamb

Preparation Time: 15 minutes
Cooking Time: 35 minutes
Servings: 5

Ingredients:

- 1 tablespoon olive oil
- 1 garlic clove, minced
- Salt and freshly ground black pepper, to taste
- 1 (1¾-pound) rack of lamb
- 1 egg
- 1 tablespoon breadcrumbs
- 3 ounces almonds, finely chopped

Preparation:

1. In a bowl, mix together the oil, garlic, salt, and black pepper.
2. Coat the rack of lamb evenly with oil mixture.
3. Crack the egg in a shallow bowl and beat well.
4. In another bowl, mix together the breadcrumbs and almonds.
5. Dip the rack of lamb in beaten egg and then, coat with almond mixture.
6. Press "Power Button" of Ninja Foodi Digital Air Fry Oven and turn the dial to select "Air Fry" mode.
7. Press "Time Button" and again turn the dial to set the cooking time to 30 minutes.
8. Now push "Temp Button" and rotate the dial to set the temperature at 220 degrees F.
9. Press "Start/Pause" button to start.
10. When the unit beeps to show that it is preheated, open the lid and grease air fry basket.
11. Place the rack of lamb into the prepared air fry basket and insert in the oven.
12. After 30 minutes, set the temperature of to 390 degrees F for 5 minutes.
13. When cooking time is complete, open the lid and place the rack of lamb onto a cutting board for about 5 minutes.
14. With a sharp knife, cut the rack of lamb into individual chops and serve.

Serving Suggestions: Serve with a fresh spinach salad.

Variation Tip: For best result, remove the silver skin from rack of lamb.

Nutritional Information per Serving:

Calories: 408|**Fat:** 26.3g|**Sat Fat:** 6.3g|**Carbohydrates:** 4.9g|**Fiber:** 2.2g|**Sugar:** 0.9g|**Protein:** 37.2g

Buttered Rib-Eye Steak

Preparation Time: 10 minutes
Cooking Time: 14 minutes
Servings: 3

Ingredients:

- 2 (8-ounce) rib-eye steaks
- 2 tablespoons butter, melted
- Salt and freshly ground black pepper, to taste

Preparation:

1. Coat the steak with butter and then sprinkle with salt and black pepper evenly.
2. Press "Power Button" of Ninja Foodi Digital Air Fry Oven and turn the dial to select "Air Roast" mode.
3. Press "Time Button" and again turn the dial to set the cooking time to 14 minutes.
4. Now push "Temp Button" and rotate the dial to set the temperature at 400 degrees F.
5. Press "Start/Pause" button to start.
6. When the unit beeps to show that it is preheated, open the lid and grease the air fry basket.
7. Arrange the steaks into the air fry basket and insert in the oven.
8. When cooking time is complete, open the lid and place steaks onto a platter for about 5 minutes.
9. Cut each steak into desired sized slices and serve.

Serving Suggestions: Enjoy this steak with grille potatoes.

Variation Tip: Rib-eye steak is best when it's cooked medium-rare.

Nutritional Information per Serving:

Calories: 383|**Fat:** 23.7g|**Sat Fat:** 10.2g|**Carbohydrates:** 0g|**Fiber:** 0g|**Sugar:** 0g|**Protein:** 41g

Bacon-Wrapped Filet Mignon

Preparation Time: 10 minutes
Cooking Time: 15 minutes
Servings: 2

Ingredients:

- 2 bacon slices
- 2 (4-ounce) filet mignon
- Salt and freshly ground black pepper, to taste
- Olive oil cooking spray

Preparation:

1. Wrap 1 bacon slice around each filet mignon and secure with toothpicks.
2. Season the filets with the salt and black pepper lightly.
3. Press "Power Button" of Ninja Foodi Digital Air Fry Oven and turn the dial to select "Air Fry" mode.
4. Press "Time Button" and again turn the dial to set the cooking time to 15 minutes.
5. Now push "Temp Button" and rotate the dial to set the temperature at 375 degrees F.
6. Press "Start/Pause" button to start.
7. When the unit beeps to show that it is preheated, open the lid.
8. Arrange the filets over the greased rack and insert in the oven.
9. Flip the filets once halfway through.
10. When cooking time is complete, open the lid and transfer the filets onto serving plates.
11. Serve hot.

Serving Suggestions: Fresh baby greens will accompany these filets greatly.

Variation Tip: Don't forget to secure the wrapped meat with toothpicks.

Nutritional Information per Serving:

Calories: 226|**Fat:** 9.5g|**Sat Fat:** g3.6|**Carbohydrates:** 0g|**Fiber:** 0g|**Sugar:** 0g|**Protein:** 33.3g

Beef Sirloin Roast

Preparation Time: 10 minutes
Cooking Time: 50 minutes
Servings: 8

Ingredients:

- 1 tablespoon smoked paprika
- 1 teaspoon ground cumin
- 1 teaspoon garlic powder
- Salt and freshly ground black pepper, to taste
- 2½ pounds sirloin roast

Preparation:

1. In a bowl, mix together the spices, salt and black pepper.
2. Rub the roast with spice mixture generously.
3. Place the sirloin roast into the greased baking pan.
4. Press "Power Button" of Ninja Foodi Digital Air Fry Oven and turn the dial to select "Air Roast" mode.
5. Press "Time Button" and again turn the dial to set the cooking time to 50 minutes.
6. Now push "Temp Button" and rotate the dial to set the temperature at 350 degrees F.
7. Press "Start/Pause" button to start.
8. When the unit beeps to show that it is preheated, open the lid and insert baking pan in the oven.
9. When cooking time is complete, open the lid and place the roast onto a platter for about 10 minutes before slicing.
10. With a sharp knife, cut the beef roast into desired sized slices and serve.

Serving Suggestions: Serve this roast with a topping of herbed butter.

Variation Tip: Rub the seasoning over the roast with your fingers, covering the entire exterior with an even layer.

Nutritional Information per Serving:

Calories: 260|**Fat:** 11.9g|**Sat Fat:** 4.4g|**Carbohydrates:** 0.4g|**Fiber:** 0.1g|**Sugar:** 0.1g|**Protein:** 38g

Fish and Seafood

Crab Rangoon

Preparation Time: 15 minutes.
Cooking Time: 5 minutes.
Servings: 6
Ingredients:

- 2 oz. imitation crab meat
- 2 oz. cream cheese
- 1½ tablespoons green onions chopped
- ½ tablespoons Worcestershire sauce
- 16 wonton wrappers
- Cooking oil for spritzing

Preparation:

1. Mix crab meat with cream cheese, green onions, and Worcestershire sauce in a bowl.
2. Spread the wonton wrapper on the working surface.
3. Divide the crab filling at the center of each wrapper then wet its edges.
4. Bring the four corners of each wrapper and pinch the edges together.
5. Place the crab Rangoon in the Ninja Air Fryer basket and spray them with cooking spray.
6. Transfer the basket to the Ninja Foodi Digital Air Fryer Oven and close the door.
7. Select "Air Crisp" mode by rotating the dial.
8. Press the TEMP button and change the value to 350 degrees F.
9. Press the TIME button and change the value to 5 minutes, then press START to begin cooking.
10. Serve warm.

Serving Suggestion: Serve the Rangoon's with tomato ketchup.

Variation Tip: Add garlic salt to the filling for more taste.

Nutritional Information Per Serving:
Calories 251 | Fat 17g | Sodium 723mg | Carbs 21g | Fiber 2.5g | Sugar 2g | Protein 7.3g

Lobster Tail

Preparation Time: 15 minutes.
Cooking Time: 6 minutes.
Servings: 4
Ingredients:

- 4 lobster tails
- 2 tablespoons butter, melted
- 1/2 teaspoon salt
- 1 teaspoon black pepper

Preparation:

1. Cut the lobster tails from the top to open the shell and place the tail in the Ninja Air Fryer basket.
2. Drizzle butter, black pepper, and salt on top.
3. Transfer the basket to the Ninja Foodi Digital Air Fryer Oven and close the door.
4. Select "Air Crisp" mode by rotating the dial.
5. Press the TEMP button and change the value to 380 degrees F.
6. Press the TIME button and change the value to 6 minutes, then press START to begin cooking.
7. Serve warm.

Serving Suggestion: Serve the lobster tail with roasted broccoli florets.

Variation Tip: Drizzle lemon garlic butter on top before cooking.

Nutritional Information Per Serving:
Calories 415 | Fat 15g |Sodium 634mg | Carbs 14.3g | Fiber 1.4g | Sugar 1g | Protein 23.3g

Baked Salmon

Preparation Time: 15 minutes

Cooking Time: 10 minutes.

Servings: 2

Ingredients:

- 2 (6 oz.) salmon fillets
- 1 teaspoon olive oil
- Salt, to taste
- Black pepper, to taste

Preparation:

1. Rub the salmon with olive oil, black pepper and salt.
2. Place the salmon in the Ninja Air Fryer basket.
3. Transfer the basket to the Ninja Foodi Digital Air Fryer Oven and close the door.
4. Select "Air Crisp" mode by rotating the dial.
5. Press the TEMP button and change the value to 360 degrees F.
6. Press the TIME button and change the value to 10 minutes, then press START to begin cooking.
7. Serve warm.

Serving Suggestion: Serve the salmon with lemon slices and fried rice.

Variation Tip: Use white pepper for a change of flavor.

Nutritional Information Per Serving:

Calories 378 | Fat 21g |Sodium 146mg | Carbs 7.1g | Fiber 0.1g | Sugar 0.4g | Protein 23g

Crusted Tilapia

Preparation Time: 15 minutes.
Cooking Time: 10 minutes.
Servings: 4
Ingredients:

- 4 Tilapia fillets
- 1/2 cup flour
- 4 oz. parmesan cheese, grated
- 2 teaspoons lemon zest
- 1 teaspoon salt
- 1 teaspoon garlic powder
- 1/2 teaspoon black pepper
- 1/2 teaspoon paprika
- 2 eggs

Preparation:

1. Spread flour in a bowl, beat eggs in another bowl and mix parmesan cheese with lemon zest, salt, black pepper, garlic powder and paprika in a shallow tray.
2. Coat the tilapia with flour, dip it in the eggs and coat with parmesan mixture.
3. Place the tilapia fillets in the Ninja sheet pan, lined with parchment paper.
4. Transfer the sheet pan to the Ninja Foodi Digital Air Fryer Oven and close the door.
5. Select "Air Roast" mode by rotating the dial.
6. Press the TEMP button and change the value to 400 degrees F.
7. Press the TIME button and change the value to 10 minutes, then press START to begin cooking.
8. Flip the fish once cooked halfway through and resume cooking.
9. Serve warm.

Serving Suggestion: Serve the tilapia with boiled eggs and fresh greens.

Variation Tip: Drizzle cheddar cheese on top for a rich taste.

Nutritional Information Per Serving:
Calories 351 | Fat 4g |Sodium 236mg | Carbs 19.1g | Fiber 0.3g | Sugar 0.1g | Protein 36g

Shrimp and Crab Casserole

Preparation Time: 15 minutes.
Cooking Time: 55 minutes.
Servings: 6
Ingredients:

- 2 (8 2/3 oz.) packages ready-to-serve long grain rice
- 1/4 cup butter, cubed
- 2 celery ribs, chopped
- 1 medium onion, chopped
- 3 tablespoons all-purpose flour
- 1 ½ cups half-and-half cream
- 3/4 teaspoon salt
- 1/2 teaspoon hot pepper sauce
- 1/4 teaspoon black pepper
- 1 teaspoon seafood seasoning
- 1 ½ lbs. shrimp, peeled and deveined
- 2 cans (6 oz.) lump crabmeat, drained
- 1 cup Colby-Monterey Jack cheese, shredded

Preparation:

1. Spread the long grain rice to a 13x9 inches baking dish.
2. Sauté celery and onion with butter in a skillet for 8 minutes.
3. Stir in flour and cream then mix well for 2 minutes.
4. Add black pepper, pepper sauce, salt and seafood seasoning.
5. Stir in shrimp, mix and spread this mixture over the rice.
6. Drizzle cheese on top and cover it a foil sheet.
7. Transfer the baking dish to the Ninja Foodi Digital Air Fryer Oven and close the door.
8. Select the "Bake" mode by rotating the dial.
9. Press the TEMP button and change the value to 350 degrees F.
10. Press the TIME button and change the value to 45 minutes, then press START to begin cooking.
11. Serve warm.

Serving Suggestion: Serve the casserole with crispy onion rings on the side.

Variation Tip: Add boiled pasta to the casserole and sliced jalapenos on top.

Nutritional Information Per Serving:
Calories 376 | Fat 17g | Sodium 1127mg | Carbs 24g | Fiber 1g | Sugar 3g | Protein 29g

Lemon Shrimp and Vegetables

Preparation Time: 15 minutes.
Cooking Time: 6 minutes.
Servings: 4
Ingredients:

- 1 cup broccoli, chopped
- 1 cup cauliflower, chopped
- 12 oz. small shrimp
- 1 tablespoons garlic and herb seasoning
- 2 tablespoons olive oil
- Juice half lemon
- Salt and black pepper, to taste

Preparation:

1. Toss shrimp and veggies in a large bowl.
2. Add garlic seasoning, olive oil, lemon juice, black pepper and salt.
3. Mix well and spread the shrimp mixture on the Ninja baking sheet.
4. Transfer the basket to the Ninja Foodi Digital Air Fryer Oven and close the door.
5. Select "Air Crisp" mode by rotating the dial.
6. Press the TEMP button and change the value to 380 degrees F.
7. Press the TIME button and change the value to 6 minutes, then press START to begin cooking.
8. Toss the shrimp and veggies once cooked halfway through and resume cooking.
9. Serve warm.

Serving Suggestion: Serve the shrimp mix with alfredo sauce on top.

Variation Tip: Add zucchini noodles to the veggies and shrimp.

Nutritional Information Per Serving:
Calories 392 | Fat 16g | Sodium 466mg | Carbs 3.9g | Fiber 0.9g | Sugar 0.6g | Protein 48g

Garlic Parmesan Shrimp

Preparation Time: 15 minutes.

Cooking Time: 12 minutes.

Servings: 4

Ingredients:

- 1 lb. shrimp, peeled and deveined
- 2 tablespoons olive oil
- ⅛ teaspoons garlic powder
- ½ teaspoons salt
- ½ teaspoons black pepper
- 2 tablespoons parmesan cheese, grated
- 2 tablespoons parsley, minced

Preparation:

1. Mix parsley, cheese, black pepper, salt, garlic powder, and olive oil in a bowl.
2. Toss in shrimp, then mix well to coat.
3. Spread the shrimp in the Ninja sheet pan.
4. Transfer the sheet pan to the Ninja Foodi Digital Air Fryer Oven and close the door.
5. Select "Air Roast" mode by rotating the dial.
6. Press the TEMP button and change the value to 350 degrees F.
7. Press the TIME button and change the value to 12 minutes, then press START to begin cooking.
8. Serve warm.

Serving Suggestion: Serve the shrimp with vegetable rice.

Variation Tip: Add canned corn to the shrimp.

Nutritional Information Per Serving:
Calories 258 | Fat 9g | Sodium 994mg | Carbs 1g | Fiber 0.4g | Sugar 3g | Protein 16g

Mangalorean Fish Fry

Preparation Time: 15 minutes.
Cooking Time: 14 minutes.
Servings: 4
Ingredients:

- 1 teaspoon black peppercorns
- 1 teaspoon coriander seeds
- 1 teaspoon cumin seeds
- 1 teaspoon turmeric
- 1-inch piece of ginger
- 3 fresh garlic cloves, minced
- 15 curry leaves
- 1 tablespoon lime juice
- 2 lbs. salmon steaks
- 2 tablespoons coconut oil
- Extra lime juice

Preparation:

1. Roast coriander, black peppercorns, and cumin in a dry skillet for 4 minutes.
2. Transfer these spices to a grinder and grind them into a powder.
3. Add ginger, garlic, turmeric, and curry leaves, then blend until smooth.
4. Rub this paste over the fish, place it in a tray, and cover the fish for 30 minutes.
5. Place the fish in the Ninja Air Fryer basket and drizzle coconut oil.
6. Transfer the basket to the Ninja Foodi Digital Air Fryer Oven and close the door.
7. Select "Air Crisp" mode by rotating the dial.
8. Press the TEMP button and change the value to 400 degrees F.
9. Press the TIME button and change the value to 10 minutes, then press START to begin cooking.
10. Flip the fish once cooked halfway through and resume cooking.
11. Garnish with lime juice.
12. Serve warm.

Serving Suggestion: Serve the salmon fillets with fried rice.

Variation Tip: Air Fry the salmon with a lemon slice on top.

Nutritional Information Per Serving:
Calories 321 | Fat 7.4g |Sodium 356mg | Carbs 9.3g | Fiber 2.4g | Sugar 5g | Protein 37.2g

Bacon Wrapped Shrimp

Preparation Time: 15 minutes.
Cooking Time: 10 minutes.
Servings: 6
Ingredients:

- 24 shrimp, deveined
- 8 bacon slices, cut into thirds
- 1 tablespoon olive oil
- 1 teaspoon paprika
- 2 garlic cloves, minced
- 1 tablespoon parsley, chopped

Preparation:

1. Mix parsley, garlic, paprika and olive oil in a large bowl.
2. Add shrimp then mix well to coat.
3. Wrap the bacon strips around each shrimp.
4. Place the wrapped shrimp, cover and refrigerate for 30 minutes.
5. Transfer the wrapped shrimp to the Air Fryer basket and spray them with cooking spray.
6. Transfer the sheet pan to the Ninja Foodi Digital Air Fryer Oven and close the door.
7. Select "Air Crisp" mode by rotating the dial.
8. Press the TEMP button and change the value to 400 degrees F.
9. Press the TIME button and change the value to 10 minutes, then press START to begin cooking.
10. Serve warm.

Serving Suggestion: Serve the shrimp with fresh greens and chili sauce on the side.

Variation Tip: Roll the wrapped shrimp in breadcrumbs for a crispy touch.

Nutritional Information Per Serving:
Calories 457 | Fat 19g |Sodium 557mg | Carbs 19g | Fiber 1.8g | Sugar 1.2g | Protein 32.5g

Cajun Shrimp

Preparation Time: 15 minutes.
Cooking Time: 8 minutes.
Servings: 4
Ingredients:

- 1 tablespoon Cajun seasoning
- 24 (1 lb.) shrimp, cleaned and peeled
- 6 oz. cooked turkey sausage, sliced
- 1 medium zucchini, sliced
- 1 medium yellow squash, sliced
- 1 red bell pepper, seeded and diced
- 1/4 teaspoon salt
- 2 tablespoons olive oil

Preparation:

1. Toss shrimp with Cajun seasoning in a large bowl.
2. Mix bell peppers, zucchini squash and sausage with oil in a bowl.
3. Spread the shrimp and veggies to the Ninja sheet pan.
4. Transfer the sheet pan to the Ninja Foodi Digital Air Fryer Oven and close the door.
5. Select "Air Roast" mode by rotating the dial.
6. Press the TEMP button and change the value to 400 degrees F.
7. Press the TIME button and change the value to 8 minutes, then press START to begin cooking.
8. Serve warm.

Serving Suggestion: Serve the shrimp meal with mashed potatoes.

Variation Tip: Spread crispy nachos at the base of the sheet pan before adding veggies and seafood.

Nutritional Information Per Serving:
Calories 378 | Fat 7g | Sodium 316mg | Carbs 16.2g | Fiber 0.3g | Sugar 0.3g | Protein 26g

Sheet Pan Shrimp Asparagus Potato

Preparation Time: 15 minutes.
Cooking Time: 44 minutes.
Servings: 4
Ingredients:

- 1 lb. shrimp peeled, deveined
- 1 lb. baby potatoes, halved
- 1 lb. asparagus trimmed
- 16 cherry tomatoes
- 3 tablespoons olive oil
- 1/2 lemon, juiced
- 1 garlic clove, minced
- 1/2 teaspoon dried parsley
- 1/8 teaspoon crushed red pepper flakes
- Sea Salt, to taste
- Black Pepper, to taste

Preparation:

1. Toss potatoes with black pepper, salt and 1 tablespoon olive oil in the Ninja sheet pan.
2. Transfer the sheet pan to the Ninja Foodi Digital Air Fryer Oven and close the door.
3. Select "Air Roast" mode by rotating the dial.
4. Press the TEMP button and change the value to 400 degrees F.
5. Press the TIME button and change the value to 12 minutes, then press START to begin cooking.
6. Meanwhile, toss tomatoes with shrimp, lemon, garlic, parsley, crushed red pepper, sea salt and 1 tablespoon olive oil in a large bowl.
7. Push the roasted potatoes aside in the sheet pan and add asparagus and shrimp mixture.
8. Drizzle black pepper, salt and olive oil over the asparagus.
9. Transfer the sheet pan to the Ninja Foodi Digital Air Fryer Oven and close the door.
10. Press the TIME button and change the value to 10 minutes, then press START to begin cooking.
11. Once it's done, switch the Ninja digital Air Fryer oven to "Air broil" mode and cook for 2 minutes.
12. Serve warm.

Serving Suggestion: Serve the shrimp meal on top of the rice risotto.

Variation Tip: Add paprika for more spice.

Nutritional Information Per Serving:
Calories 448 | Fat 13g | Sodium 353mg | Carbs 31g | Fiber 0.4g | Sugar 1g | Protein 29g

Vegetables and Sides

Kale and Potato Nuggets

Preparation Time: 15 minutes.

Cooking Time: 45 minutes.

Servings: 6

Ingredients:

- 2 cups potatoes, chopped
- 1 teaspoon olive oil
- 1 garlic clove, minced
- 4 cups kale, chopped
- 1/8 cup almond milk
- 1/4 teaspoon sea salt
- 1/8 teaspoon black pepper
- Cooking oil spray

Preparation:

1. Boil potatoes in boiling water in a cooking pot for 30 minutes, then drain.
2. Sauté garlic with oil in a skillet for 1 minute.
3. Stir in kale and cook for 3 minutes, then transfer to a bowl.
4. Mash boiled potatoes in a medium bowl, then milk, black pepper, and salt.
5. Mix well, then add kale mixture and stir well.
6. Make 1-inch nuggets out of this mixture and place the nuggets in the Ninja Air Fryer basket, then coat them with cooking oil.
7. Transfer the basket to the Ninja Foodi Digital Air Fryer Oven and close the door.
8. Select "Air Crisp" mode by rotating the dial.
9. Press the TEMP button and change the value to 400 degrees F.
10. Press the TIME button and change the value to 12 minutes, then press START to begin cooking.
11. Toss the nuggets once cooked halfway through and resume cooking.
12. Serve warm.

Serving Suggestion: Serve the potato nuggets with pita bread and chili sauce.

Variation Tip: Add boiled and mashed chickpeas to the batter

Nutritional Information Per Serving:
Calories 338 | Fat 24g |Sodium 620mg | Carbs 58.3g | Fiber 2.4g | Sugar 1.2g | Protein 5.4g

Loaded Tater Tots

Preparation Time: 15 minutes.
Cooking Time: 25 minutes.
Servings: 4
Ingredients:

- 2 lbs. frozen tater tots
- 1/2 cup crumbled feta cheese
- 1/4 cup red onion, peeled, diced
- 1/4 cup black olives, sliced
- Fresh dill, for garnish

Tzatziki Sauce

- 1 cup Greek yogurt
- 1 English cucumber, grated
- 3 garlic cloves, peeled, minced
- 2 tablespoons fresh lemon juice
- 3 tablespoons fresh dill, chopped
- 1 teaspoon salt
- 1 teaspoon black pepper

Preparation:

1. Prepare the tzatziki sauce by mixing all the ingredients in a bowl.
2. Cover and refrigerate the sauce until the tater tots are ready.
3. Spread the tater tots in the Ninja Air Fryer basket.
4. Transfer the basket to the Ninja Foodi Digital Air Fryer Oven and close the door.
5. Select "Air Crisp" mode by rotating the dial.
6. Press the TEMP button and change the value to 450 degrees F.
7. Press the TIME button and change the value to 15 minutes, then press START to begin cooking.
8. Transfer the tater tots to the Ninja sheet pan.
9. Add feta cheese, olives, and red onion on top.
10. Return the sheet pan to the Ninja digital Air Fryer oven.
11. Select the "Bake" mode by rotating the dial.
12. Press the TEMP button and change the value to 350 degrees F.
13. Press the TIME button and change the value to 10 minutes, then press START to begin cooking.
14. Serve the tater tots with the tzatziki sauce.

Serving Suggestion: Serve the tater tots with guacamole on top.

Variation Tip: Add olives or sliced mushrooms.

Nutritional Information Per Serving:
Calories 246 | Fat 15g | Sodium 220mg | Carbs 40.3g | Fiber 2.4g | Sugar 1.2g | Protein 12.4g

Eggplant Parmesan

Preparation Time: 15 minutes.
Cooking Time: 25 minutes.
Servings: 4
Ingredients:

- 2 eggs
- 1 tablespoon water
- 1 cup panko breadcrumbs
- 1/4 cup grated parmesan cheese
- 1 teaspoon dried oregano
- 1 teaspoon dried basil
- 1/2 teaspoon garlic powder
- 2 tablespoons olive oil
- 1 eggplant, cut into ¼ -inch thick slices
- 1 (25 oz.) jar marinara sauce
- 8 oz. mozzarella cheese, shredded
- julienned fresh basil,

Preparation:

1. Place the eggplant in a colander and drizzle salt on top. Leave it for 15 minutes to drain excess water.
2. Pat dry the eggplant slices and place them on a plate.
3. Mix panko breadcrumbs with dried oregano, garlic powder, dried basil, and parmesan cheese in a shallow tray.
4. Beat eggs with water in a shallow bowl.
5. First, dip the eggplant slices in the egg wash, then coat them with breadcrumbs mixture.
6. Place the eggplant slices in the Ninja sheet pan and drizzle olive oil on top.
7. Transfer the sheet pan to the Ninja Foodi Digital Air Fryer Oven and close the door.
8. Select the "Bake" mode by rotating the dial.
9. Press the TEMP button and change the value to 350 degrees F.
10. Press the TIME button and change the value to 15 minutes, then press START to begin cooking.
11. Flip the eggplant slices and drizzle mozzarella cheese on top.
12. Continue baking these slices for 10 minutes in the Ninja digital Air Fryer oven.
13. Serve warm.

Serving Suggestion: Serve the eggplant with spaghetti or any other pasta.

Variation Tip: Top the eggplant slice with a pepperoni slice before adding cheese and cooking.

Nutritional Information Per Serving:
Calories 341 | Fat 24g |Sodium 547mg | Carbs 36.4g | Fiber 1.2g | Sugar 1g | Protein 10.3g

Tofu Butternut Squash Dinner

Preparation Time: 15 minutes.

Cooking Time: 20 minutes.

Servings: 6

Ingredients:

- 1 package sprouted tofu, diced
- 12 oz. frozen butternut squash. cubed
- 12 oz. frozen pearl onions
- 1 red bell pepper, cut into chunks
- 3 frozen garlic cubes
- 12 oz. frozen broccoli florets

Preparation:

1. Toss tofu, butternut cubes, pearl onions, red bell pepper, garlic cubes, and broccoli florets in a bowl.
2. Spread the veggies and tofu in the Ninja sheet pan.
3. Transfer the sheet pan to the Ninja Foodi Digital Air Fryer Oven and close the door.
4. Select the "Bake" mode by rotating the dial.
5. Press the TEMP button and change the value to 400 degrees F.
6. Press the TIME button and change the value to 20 minutes, then press START to begin cooking.
7. Serve warm.

Serving Suggestion: Serve the tofu with roasted mushrooms.

Variation Tip: Add lemon zest and lemon juice for better taste.

Nutritional Information Per Serving:

Calories 324 | Fat 5g |Sodium 432mg | Carbs 13.1g | Fiber 0.3g | Sugar 1g | Protein 5.7g

Sheet Pan Tofu Dinner

Preparation Time: 15 minutes.
Cooking Time: 30 minutes.
Servings: 4
Ingredients:

- 1 (14-oz.) package tofu, cut into cubes
- 2 medium carrots, peeled and cut into chunks
- 1 small head cauliflower, florets
- 1 medium sweet potato, peeled and diced
- 1 small red onion, quartered
- 1 small bunch asparagus, trimmed
- 4 tablespoons olive oil
- Salt, to taste
- Black pepper, to taste

Preparation:

1. Season the tofu with black pepper, salt and oil in a bowl.
2. Mix carrots, cauliflower, sweet potato, red onion, olive oil, salt and black pepper in a bowl for seasoning
3. Spread tofu and veggies in the Ninja sheet pan.
4. Transfer the sheet pan to the Ninja Foodi Digital Air Fryer Oven and close the door.
5. Select "Air Roast" mode by rotating the dial.
6. Press the TEMP button and change the value to 425 degrees F.
7. Press the TIME button and change the value to 15 minutes, then press START to begin cooking.
8. Toss asparagus with olive oil, black pepper, and salt.
9. Add this asparagus to the Ninja sheet pan and return it to the Ninja digital Air Fryer oven.
10. Continue baking the veggies for 15 minutes.
11. Serve warm.

Serving Suggestion: Serve the tofu dinner with crispy nachos and mashed potatoes.

Variation Tip: Add crispy dried onion for better taste.

Nutritional Information Per Serving:
Calories 304 | Fat 31g |Sodium 834mg | Carbs 21.4g | Fiber 0.2g | Sugar 0.3g | Protein 4.6g

Spicy Cauliflower Stir-Fry

Preparation Time: 15 minutes.
Cooking Time: 20 minutes.
Servings: 4
Ingredients:

- 1 head cauliflower, florets
- ¾ cup onion white, sliced
- 5 garlic cloves, sliced
- 1 ½ tablespoons tamari
- 1 tablespoon rice vinegar
- ½ teaspoon coconut sugar
- 1 tablespoon Sriracha
- 2 scallions for garnish

Preparation:

1. Spread the cauliflower in the Ninja Air Fryer basket.
2. Transfer the basket to the Ninja Foodi Digital Air Fryer Oven and close the door.
3. Select "Air Crisp" mode by rotating the dial.
4. Press the TEMP button and change the value to 350 degrees F.
5. Press the TIME button and change the value to 10 minutes, then press START to begin cooking.
6. Add sliced onion and garlic to the cauliflower to Air Frye for 5 minutes.
7. Meanwhile, mix black pepper, salt, sriracha, coconut sugar, and rice vinegar in a bowl.
8. Pour this mixture over the cauliflower and onion, then cook for 5 minutes.
9. Garnish with scallions.
10. Serve warm.

Serving Suggestion: Serve the cauliflower with lemon wedges.

Variation Tip: Add breadcrumbs to the florets before baking for a crispy texture.

Nutritional Information Per Serving:
Calories 93 | Fat 3g |Sodium 510mg | Carbs 12g | Fiber 3g | Sugar 4g | Protein 4g

Porcini Mac and Cheese

Preparation Time: 15 minutes.
Cooking Time: 60 minutes.
Servings: 8
Ingredients:

- 1 (1 oz.) package dried porcini mushrooms
- 1 cup boiling water
- 1 (16 oz.) package pasta shells
- 6 tablespoons butter, cubed
- 1 cup baby portobello mushrooms, chopped
- 1 shallot, chopped
- 1 garlic clove, minced
- 3 tablespoons all-purpose flour
- 2 ½ cups milk
- 1/2 cup pumpkin ale
- 2 cups cheddar cheese, shredded
- 1 cup shredded fontina cheese
- 1 teaspoon salt
- 1 cup bread crumbs

Preparation:

1. Soak dried mushroom in boiling water for 20 minutes, then drain.
2. Boil pasta as per the cooking instructions and drain.
3. Sauté portobello mushrooms with butter and shallot in a Dutch oven for 3 minutes.
4. Stir in garlic then sauté for 1 minute then add flour, beer and milk.
5. Mix and cook for 4 minutes until the mixture thickens.
6. Stir in cheese, salt, dried mushrooms and mix well then spread the mixture in a 13x9inches casserole dish.
7. Transfer the casserole dish to the Ninja Foodi Digital Air Fryer Oven and close the door.
8. Select the "Bake" mode by rotating the dial.
9. Press the TEMP button and change the value to 350 degrees F.
10. Press the TIME button and change the value to 35 minutes, then press START to begin cooking.
11. Serve warm.

Serving Suggestion: Serve the mac and cheese with roasted veggies on the side.

Variation Tip: Add canned corn to the casserole.

Nutritional Information Per Serving:
Calories 351 | Fat 19g |Sodium 412mg | Carbs 43g | Fiber 0.3g | Sugar 1g | Protein 23g

Herbed Potato, Asparagus, and Chickpea

Preparation Time: 15 minutes.
Cooking Time: 35 minutes.
Servings: 4
Ingredients:

- 1 lb. baby potatoes, sliced
- 1 ½ cups baby carrots
- 1 can (14oz.) chickpeas, drained and rinsed
- 1 teaspoon dried basil
- 1 teaspoon dried thyme
- 1 teaspoon dried oregano
- 1 teaspoon paprika
- ½ teaspoon garlic powder
- 3 tablespoons olive oil
- 1 lb. asparagus, trimmed and cut into thirds
- ½ large yellow onion, sliced
- Salt and black pepper, to taste
- Fresh parsley, to serve

Preparation:

1. Toss chickpeas, carrots, and potatoes with 1 ½ tablespoon oil and ¾ spices in a large bowl.
2. Spread the mixture in the Ninja sheet pan.
3. Transfer the sheet pan to the Ninja Foodi Digital Air Fryer Oven and close the door.
4. Select "Air Roast" mode by rotating the dial.
5. Press the TEMP button and change the value to 425 degrees F.
6. Press the TIME button and change the value to 25 minutes, then press START to begin cooking.
7. Toss asparagus and onion with rest of the ingredients in a tray.
8. Add these veggies to the sheet pan and return it to the Ninja digital Air Fryer oven.
9. Cook for another 15 minutes.
10. Serve warm.

Serving Suggestion: Serve the veggies with white rice or spaghetti squash.

Variation Tip: Add green beans instead of asparagus.

Nutritional Information Per Serving:
Calories 318 | Fat 15.7g | Sodium 124mg | Carbs 27g | Fiber 0.1g | Sugar 0.3g | Protein 4.9g

Kale Salad with Roasted Veggies

Preparation Time: 15 minutes.
Cooking Time: 23 minutes.
Servings: 4
Ingredients:

- 6 tablespoons olive oil
- 2 tablespoons balsamic vinegar
- 1 tablespoon tamari
- 2 garlic cloves, smashed
- ½ teaspoon dried basil
- ½ teaspoon dried rosemary
- 1 tablespoons shallot, chopped
- Black pepper, to taste
- Juice of 1 lemon
- 10 oz. baby Bella mushrooms, quartered
- 1-pint grape tomatoes
- 2 medium zucchinis, diced
- 1 medium red onion, diced
- Salt, to taste
- 1 bunch green kale, roughly chopped
- ½ cup parmesan cheese, grated

Preparation:

1. Toss mushrooms with garlic, tamari, 1 tablespoon balsamic, 2 tablespoons olive oil, black pepper, lemon juice, and dried herbs in a bowl.
2. Cover and refrigerate the mixture for 30 minutes.
3. Meanwhile, mix zucchini, onion and tomatoes with 3 tablespoons in a bowl.
4. Spread the veggies and marinated mushrooms to the Ninja sheet pan.
5. Transfer the sheet pan to the Ninja Foodi Digital Air Fryer Oven and close the door.
6. Select the "Bake" mode by rotating the dial.
7. Press the TEMP button and change the value to 425 degrees F.
8. Press the TIME button and change the value to 20 minutes, then press START to begin cooking.
9. Toss the veggies once cooked halfway through and resume cooking.
10. Meanwhile, mix kale with salt in a bowl, then sauté with 1 tablespoon olive oil, lemon juice, and balsamic vinegar in a pan for 3 minutes.
11. Toss the veggies with kales in a salad bowl.
12. Drizzle parmesan cheese on top.
13. Serve.

Serving Suggestion: Serve the kale salad with mashed potatoes.

Variation Tip: Add boiled couscous to the salad.

Nutritional Information Per Serving:
Calories 378 | Fat 3.8g |Sodium 620mg | Carbs 13.3g | Fiber 2.4g | Sugar 1.2g | Protein 5.4g

Sheet Pan Fajitas

Preparation Time: 15 minutes.

Cooking Time: 15 minutes.

Servings: 6

Ingredients:

- 3 bell peppers, sliced
- 1 large yellow onion, sliced
- 1 (15oz.) can pinto beans, drained, rinsed
- 1 tablespoon olive oil
- 1/4 teaspoon paprika
- 1/4 teaspoon garlic powder
- 1/4 teaspoon cumin
- 1/4 teaspoon salt
- 1/4 cup cheddar cheese, shredded
- Tortillas for serving

Preparation:

1. Spread the pinto beans in the Ninja Sheet pan, lined with parchment paper.
2. Top the beans with bell peppers, yellow onion, olive oil, paprika, garlic powder, cumin, salt, and cheese
3. Transfer the sheet pan to the Ninja Foodi Digital Air Fryer Oven and close the door.
4. Select the "Bake" mode by rotating the dial.
5. Press the TEMP button and change the value to 350 degrees F.
6. Press the TIME button and change the value to 15 minutes, then press START to begin cooking.
7. Serve in tortillas.

Serving Suggestion: Serve the nachos with tomato sauce or guacamole.

Variation Tip: Add crushed tomatoes for a saucy texture.

Nutritional Information Per Serving:
Calories 391 | Fat 2.2g |Sodium 276mg | Carbs 27.7g | Fiber 0.9g | Sugar 1.4g | Protein 8.8g

Artichoke Spinach Casserole

Preparation Time: 15 minutes.
Cooking Time: 35 minutes.
Servings: 8
Ingredients:

- 1 lb. mushrooms, sliced
- 1/3 cup chicken broth
- 1 tablespoon all-purpose flour
- ½ cup evaporated milk
- 4 (10 oz.) packages spinach, thawed
- 2 cans (14 oz.) artichoke hearts, drained and sliced
- 1 cup sour cream
- ½ cup mayonnaise
- 3 tablespoons lemon juice
- ½ teaspoon garlic powder
- ¼ teaspoon salt
- 2 cans (14 ½ oz.) tomatoes, diced and drained
- ¼ teaspoon black pepper
- Paprika, for topping

Preparation:

1. Cook mushrooms with broth in a cooking pot for 3 minutes. Transfer the mushrooms to a plate using a slotted spoon.
2. Mix flour with milk in a bowl until smooth.
3. Pour this mixture into the broth and cook for 2 minutes until the mixture thickens.
4. Add tomatoes, mushrooms and spinach to the sauce.
5. Spread the artichoke hearts in a 13x9 inches casserole dish.
6. Add the spinach mixture on top.
7. Whisk sour cream with lemon juice, mayonnaise, salt, black pepper and garlic powder in a bowl.
8. Spread this mayo mixture on top and drizzle paprika on top.
9. Transfer the casserole dish to the Ninja Foodi Digital Air Fryer Oven and close the door.
10. Select the "Bake" mode by rotating the dial.
11. Press the TEMP button and change the value to 350 degrees F.
12. Press the TIME button and change the value to 30 minutes, then press START to begin cooking.
13. Serve warm.

Serving Suggestion: Serve the casserole with sautéed asparagus and toasted bread slices.

Variation Tip: Add boiled pasta to the casserole.

Nutritional Information Per Serving:
Calories 136 | Fat 10g | Sodium 249mg | Carbs 8g | Fiber 2g | Sugar 3g | Protein 4g

Dessert Recipes

Molten Lava Cake

Preparation Time: 15 minutes.
Cooking Time: 12 minutes.
Servings: 6
Ingredients:

- 8 oz. chocolate, shredded
- 10 tablespoons butter
- 3 large eggs
- 3 egg yolks
- 1/2 teaspoon salt
- 1 1/2 cups powdered sugar
- 1/2 cup all-purpose flour

Preparation:

1. Grease six- 6 oz. ramekins with cooking spray.
2. Melt chocolate and butter in a glass bowl by heating in the microwave for 2 minutes.
3. Stir in flour, sugar and salt then mix well until it makes a smooth dough.
4. Stir in egg yolks and eggs then mix well.
5. Divide this batter in the ramekins and place them in the sheet pan.

Transfer the sheet pan to the Ninja Foodi Digital Air Fryer Oven and close the door.

6. Select the "Bake" mode by rotating the dial.
7. Press the TEMP button and change the value to 400 degrees F.
8. Press the TIME button and change the value to 10 minutes, then press START to begin cooking.
9. Allow the ramekins to cool then garnish with berries, sugar, and cream.
10. Serve.

Serving Suggestion: Serve the cakes with cream frosting on top.

Variation Tip: Add chocolate chips or a tsp of crushed nuts to the batter for the change of flavor.

Nutritional Information Per Serving:
Calories 245 | Fat 14g | Sodium 122mg | Carbs 23.3g | Fiber 1.2g | Sugar 12g | Protein 4.3g

Sweet Apples

Preparation Time: 15 minutes.
Cooking Time: 9 minutes.
Servings: 6
Ingredients:

- 6 apples, cored and diced
- ¼ cup brown sugar
- ¼ cup white sugar
- ¼ teaspoon ground cloves
- ¼ teaspoon pumpkin pie spice
- ½ teaspoon ground cinnamon
- ⅓ cup of water

Preparation:

1. Mix water with cloves, pie spice, cinnamon, white sugar, and brown sugar in a saucepan.
2. Cook this sugar mixture for 2 minutes until it thickens.
3. Toss in apples, mix well to coat then spread them in the Ninja Air Fryer basket.
4. Transfer the basket to the Ninja Foodi Digital Air Fryer Oven and close the door.
5. Select "Air Crips" mode by rotating the dial.
6. Press the TEMP button and change the value to 350 degrees F.
7. Press the TIME button and change the value to 6 minutes, then press START to begin cooking.
8. Allow the apples to cool then serve.

Serving Suggestion: Serve the apples with sweet cream cheese dip.

Variation Tip: Use apple sauce to season the apples.

Nutritional Information Per Serving:
Calories 153 | Fat 1g | Sodium 8mg | Carbs 66g | Fiber 0.8g | Sugar 56g | Protein 1g

Carrot Cake

Preparation Time: 15 minutes.

Cooking Time: 30 minutes.

Servings: 8

Ingredients:

- 5 oz. brown sugar
- 2 eggs, beaten
- 5 oz. butter
- 1 orange, zest, and juice
- 7 oz. self-rising flour
- 1 teaspoon ground cinnamon
- 2 medium carrots, grated
- 20 oz. sultanas

Preparation:

1. Beat eggs in a mixing bowl and stir in sugar, and butter then beat until sugar is dissolved.
2. Stir in flour and mix until it makes a smooth batter.
3. Fold in sultanas, grated carrots, orange juice, and orange zest.
4. Mix well, then spread this batter in a greased baking dish.
5. Transfer the baking dish to the Ninja Foodi Digital Air Fryer Oven and close the door.
6. Select the "Bake" mode by rotating the dial.
7. Press the TEMP button and change the value to 350 degrees F.
8. Press the TIME button and change the value to 30 minutes, then press START to begin cooking.
9. Once done, allow the cake to cool.
10. Slice and serve.

Serving Suggestion: Serve the cake with creamy frosting on top.

Variation Tip: Add chopped pecans or walnuts to the batter.

Nutritional Information Per Serving:
Calories 195 | Fat 3g |Sodium 355mg | Carbs 20g | Fiber 1g | Sugar 25g | Protein 1g

Strawberry Roll Cake

Preparation Time: 15 minutes.
Cooking Time: 12 minutes.
Servings: 8
Ingredients:

Sponge Cake

- ½ cup sugar
- 4 large eggs
- ¾ cup all-purpose flour
- 1 teaspoon vanilla extract

Filling:

- ½ cup heavy whipping cream
- 1 cup butter salted
- 1 cup confectioner sugar
- 2 teaspoons vanilla extract
- 8 oz. strawberry preserves

Preparation:

1. Beat eggs with sugar in the bowl of a stand mixer until fluffy and pale.
2. Stir in all-purpose flour and vanilla extract, then mix well for 5 minutes until smooth.
3. Grease a 13x13 inch baking pan with butter and layer it with parchment paper.
4. Spread the batter in the baking pan.
5. Transfer the baking pan to the Ninja Foodi Digital Air Fryer Oven and close the door.
6. Select the "Bake" mode by rotating the dial.
7. Press the TEMP button and change the value to 325 degrees F.
8. Press the TIME button and change the value to 12 minutes, then press START to begin cooking.
9. Allow the sponge cake to cool, then transfer to a working surface.
10. Beat cream, butter, vanilla, and sugar in a mixer until fluffy.
11. Spread a layer of prepared buttercream on top of the cake and top it with strawberry preserves.
12. Roll the cake and slice it into 2-inch-thick slices.
13. Serve.

Serving Suggestion: Serve the sponge cake roll with fresh berries on top.

Variation Tip: Add blueberry preserves to the fillings.

Nutritional Information Per Serving:
Calories 118 | Fat 20g | Sodium 192mg | Carbs 23.7g | Fiber 0.9g | Sugar 19g | Protein 5.2g

Bread Pudding

Preparation Time: 15 minutes.

Cooking Time: 15 minutes.

Servings: 6

Ingredients:

- 2 cups bread, cubed
- 1 egg
- 2/3 cup heavy cream
- 1/2 teaspoon vanilla extract
- 1/4 cup sugar
- 1/4 cup chocolate chips

Preparation:

1. Beat egg with sugar, vanilla, and cream in a bowl.
2. Spread bread cubes and chocolate chips in the Ninja baking dish.
3. Pour the egg-sugar mixture over the bread cubes.
4. Transfer the baking dish to the Ninja Foodi Digital Air Fryer Oven and close the door.
5. Select the "Bake" mode by rotating the dial.
6. Press the TEMP button and change the value to 350 degrees F.
7. Press the TIME button and change the value to 15 minutes, then press START to begin cooking.
8. Allow the pudding to cool, then slice.
9. Serve.

Serving Suggestion: Serve the pudding with chocolate syrup on top.

Variation Tip: Add dried raisins instead of chocolate chips.

Nutritional Information Per Serving:

Calories 203 | Fat 8.9g |Sodium 340mg | Carbs 24.7g | Fiber 1.2g | Sugar 11.3g | Protein 5.3g

French Toast Sticks with Berries

Preparation Time: 15 minutes.
Cooking Time: 10 minutes.
Servings: 4
Ingredients:

- 4 (1 ½ oz.) whole-grain bread slices
- 2 large eggs
- 1/4 cup milk
- 1 teaspoon vanilla extract
- 1/2 teaspoon ground cinnamon
- 1/4 cup packed light brown sugar
- 2/3 cup flax seed meal
- Cooking spray
- 2 cups sliced fresh strawberries
- 8 teaspoons pure maple syrup
- 1 teaspoon powdered sugar

Preparation:

1. Cut the bread slices into 4 sticks and keep them aside.
2. Beat eggs with 1 tablespoon sugar, cinnamon, vanilla, and milk in a bowl.
3. Whisk flaxseed with 3 tablespoons sugar in a shallow tray.
4. Dip each breadstick in the egg mixture and coat them with a flaxseed mixture.
5. Place the coated breadsticks in the Ninja baking tray.
6. Transfer the basket to the Ninja Foodi Digital Air Fryer Oven and close the door.
7. Select "Air Crisp" mode by rotating the dial.
8. Press the TEMP button and change the value to 375 degrees F.
9. Press the TIME button and change the value to 10 minutes, then press START to begin cooking.
10. Flip the bread once cooked halfway through, then resume cooking.
11. Toss strawberries with maple syrup and sugar in a bowl.
12. Serve the French sticks with strawberry mixture.
13. Enjoy.

Serving Suggestion: Serve the bread slices with chocolate dip.

Variation Tip: Skip the flaxseed meal if not available and directly cook the French toasts after egg-milk coating.

Nutritional Information Per Serving:
Calories 361 | Fat 10g | Sodium 218mg | Carbs 56g | Fiber 10g | Sugar 30g | Protein 14g

Fudgy Brownies

Preparation Time: 15 minutes.
Cooking Time: 35 minutes.
Servings: 8
Ingredients:

- ¾ cup butter salted
- 1¾ cup dark chocolate chips
- 1 teaspoon espresso powder
- ¾ teaspoons sea salt
- 1½ cups sugar
- 5 large eggs
- ⅓ cup cooking oil
- 2 teaspoons vanilla extract
- ½ cup of cocoa powder
- 1½ cups all-purpose flour

Preparation:

1. Blend eggs, oil, sugar, and butter in a stand mixer for 3 minutes.
2. Melt 1 cup chocolate chips in a bowl by heating in the microwave.
3. Add the melted chocolate, flour, espresso powder, cocoa powder, and vanilla.
4. Mix well until it makes a batter, then fold in the remaining chocolate chips.
5. Spread the batter in an 11 ½ x 9 inches baking pan, lined with parchment paper.
6. Transfer the baking dish to the Ninja Foodi Digital Air Fryer Oven and close the door.
7. Select the "Bake" mode by rotating the dial.
8. Press the TEMP button and change the value to 325 degrees F.
9. Press the TIME button and change the value to 35 minutes, then press START to begin cooking.
10. Once done, remove the fudge from the pan and allow it to cool.
11. Slice and serve.

Serving Suggestion: Serve the fudge brownie with a scoop of vanilla cream on top.

Variation Tip: Add chopped nuts to the batter.

Nutritional Information Per Serving:
Calories 248 | Fat 16g | Sodium 95mg | Carbs 38.4g | Fiber 0.3g | Sugar 10g | Protein 14.1g

Glazed Donut

Preparation Time: 15 minutes.
Cooking Time: 15 minutes.
Servings: 10
Ingredients:

- 1 cup warm milk
- 2-1/2 teaspoons active dry yeast
- 1/4 cup 1 teaspoon granulated sugar
- 1/2 teaspoon salt
- 1 whole egg
- 1/4 cup unsalted butter, melted
- 3 cups all-purpose flour
- Cooking oil spray

Glaze

- 3 tablespoons unsalted butter
- 1 cup powdered sugar
- 1 teaspoon pure vanilla extract
- 2 tablespoons boiled water

Preparation:

1. Mix yeast with warm milk in a large bowl and leave it for 10 minutes.
2. Stir in sugar, salt, butter, and egg, then beat until sugar is dissolved.
3. Add flour, then mix until it makes a smooth dough.
4. Knead this dough for 5 minutes, place it in a greased bowl then cover with a plastic wrap.
5. Leave the dough for 1 hour, then punch it down.
6. Roll the dough into a ½ inch thick sheet and cut the 12 donuts out of this dough.
7. Place the donuts in a Ninja sheet pan lined with parchment paper.
8. Cover the donuts with a kitchen towel and leave them for 30 minutes.
9. Brush the top of the donuts with cooking oil.
10. Transfer the sheet pan to the Ninja Foodi Digital Air Fryer Oven and close the door.
11. Select the "Bake" mode by rotating the dial.
12. Press the TEMP button and change the value to 350 degrees F.
13. Press the TIME button and change the value to 10 minutes, then press START to begin cooking.
14. Meanwhile, mix the ingredients donut glaze ingredients in a saucepan.
15. Stir and cook for 5 minutes, then allow it to cool.
16. Brush the baked donuts with this glaze and leave them for 10 minutes.
17. Serve.

Serving Suggestion: Serve the donuts with chocolate or apple sauce.

Variation Tip: Dip the donuts in chocolate syrup.

Nutritional Information Per Serving:
Calories 117 | Fat 12g |Sodium 79mg | Carbs 24.8g | Fiber 1.1g | Sugar 18g | Protein 5g

Cinnamon Rolls

Preparation Time: 15 minutes.
Cooking Time: 9 minutes.
Servings: 8
Ingredients:

- 1 lb. bread dough, thawed
- ¼ cup butter, melted
- ¾ cup brown sugar
- 1½ tablespoons cinnamon ground

Cream cheese glaze

- 4 oz. cream cheese softened
- 2 tablespoons butter, softened
- 1¼ cups powdered sugar
- ½ teaspoon vanilla

Preparation:

1. Roll the bread dough on a floured surface into a 13x11 inches rectangle.
2. Brush its top with melted butter and drizzle cinnamon and sugar on top.
3. Roll the rectangle and slice the roll into 1-inch slices.
4. Place the roll in the Ninja sheet pan, greased with cooking oil.
5. Transfer the sheet to the Ninja Foodi Digital Air Fryer Oven and close the door.
6. Select the "Bake" mode by rotating the dial.
7. Press the TEMP button and change the value to 350 degrees F.
8. Press the TIME button and change the value to 9 minutes, then press START to begin cooking.
9. Beat cream cheese with butter, sugar, and vanilla in a bowl.
10. Serve the cinnamon rolls with cream cheese mixture on top.
11. Enjoy.

Serving Suggestion: Serve the cinnamon rolls with chocolate syrup on top.

Variation Tip: Add crushed walnuts or pecans to the filling.

Nutritional Information Per Serving:
Calories 198 | Fat 14g | Sodium 272mg | Carbs 34g | Fiber 1g | Sugar 9.3g | Protein 1.3g

Crispy Oreos

Preparation Time: 15 minutes.
Cooking Time: 8 minutes.
Servings: 8
Ingredients:

- 1 can crescents dough
- 8 Oreo cookies
- 2 tablespoons sugar

Preparation:

1. Spread the crescents dough on the working surface.
2. Cut the dough into 8 rounds and place the one cookie into each round.
3. Wrap the dough around the cookies and place them in the Ninja Air Fryer basket.
4. Transfer the cookies to the Ninja Foodi Digital Air Fryer Oven and close the door.
5. Select "Air Crisp" mode by rotating the dial.
6. Press the TEMP button and change the value to 350 degrees F.
7. Press the TIME button and change the value to 8 minutes, then press START to begin cooking.
8. Flip the cookies once cooked halfway through, then resume cooking.
9. Allow the cookies to cool then garnish with sugar.
10. Serve.

Serving Suggestion: Serve the Oreos with chocolate sauce.

Variation Tip: Roll the dough wrapped Oreos in crushed nuts or coconut flakes before cooking.

Nutritional Information Per Serving:
Calories 159 | Fat 3g |Sodium 277mg | Carbs 21g | Fiber 1g | Sugar 9g | Protein 2g

3 Weeks Meal Plan:

Week 1

Day 1:

Breakfast: Ham Brie Sandwich

Lunch: Bacon Wrapped Shrimp

Snack: Sweet Potato Fries

Dinner: Italian Pasta Bake

Dessert: Molten Lava Cake

Day 2:

Breakfast: Breakfast Hash

Lunch: Sheet Pan Tofu Dinner

Snack: Turkey Croquettes

Dinner: Sausage Casserole

Dessert: Crispy Oreos

Day 3:

Breakfast: Breakfast Frittata

Lunch: Eggplant Parmesan

Snack: Pork Meatballs

Dinner: Christmas Casserole

Dessert: Cinnamon Rolls

Day 4:

Breakfast: Chile-Cheese Frittata

Lunch: Herbed Potato, Asparagus, and Chickpea

Snack: Crab Rangoon

Dinner: Bacon Meatloaf

Dessert: Sweet Apples

Day 5:

Breakfast: Hasselback Potatoes

Lunch: Porcini Mac and Cheese

Snack: Spanakopita Bites

Dinner: Steak Bites Mushrooms

Dessert: Bread Pudding

Day 6:

Breakfast: Morning Bagels

Lunch: Spicy Cauliflower Stir-Fry

Snack: Pork Dumplings

Dinner: Glazed Steaks

Dessert: Carrot Cake

Day 7:

Breakfast: Egg Avocado Boats

Lunch: Sheet Pan Fajitas

Snack: Kale Salad with Roasted Veggies

Dinner: Herbed Lamb Chops

Dessert: Glazed Donut

Week 2

Day 1:

Breakfast: Ham Brie Sandwich

Lunch: Italian Turkey Breast

Snack: Sweet Potato Fries

Dinner: Lobster Tail

Dessert: Molten Lava Cake

Day 2:

Breakfast: Breakfast Hash

Lunch: Thanksgiving Turkey Meal

Snack: Corn on the Cob

Dinner: Garlic Parmesan Shrimp

Dessert: Crispy Oreos

Day 3:

Breakfast: Breakfast Frittata

Lunch: Turkey Meatloaf

Snack: Calzones

Dinner: Cajun Shrimp

Dessert: Cinnamon Rolls

Day 4:

Breakfast: Chile-Cheese Frittata

Lunch: General Tso's Chicken

Snack: Pita Pizzas

Dinner: Mangalorean Fish Fry

Dessert: Sweet Apples

Day 5:

Breakfast: Hasselback Potatoes

Snack: Spanakopita Bites

Lunch: Chicken Enchiladas

Dinner: Lemon Shrimp and Vegetables

Dessert: Bread Pudding

Day 6:

Breakfast: Morning Bagels

Lunch: Korean Chicken Wings

Snack: Pork Dumplings

Dinner: Shrimp and Crab Casserole

Dessert: Carrot Cake

Day 7:

Breakfast: Egg Avocado Boats

Lunch: Cheesy Chicken Nachos

Snack: Curry Chickpeas

Dinner: Crusted Tilapia

Dessert: Glazed Donut

Week 3

Day 1:

Breakfast: Breakfast Bombs

Lunch: Artichoke Spinach Casserole

Snack: Kale and Potato Nuggets

Dinner: Lamb Chops with Garlic Sauce

Dessert: French Toast Sticks with Berries

Day 2:

Breakfast: Egg Avocado Boats

Lunch: Chicken, Sweet Potatoes and Broccoli

Snack: Cinnamon Apple Chips

Dinner: Lamb Sirloin Steak

Dessert: Fudgy Brownies

Day 3:

Breakfast: Chile-Cheese Frittata

Lunch: Chicken Sheet Pan Meal

Snack: Corn Dog Bites

Dinner: Tofu Butternut Squash Dinner

Dessert: Strawberry Roll Cake

Day 4:

Breakfast: Chile-Cheese Frittata

Lunch: General Tso's Chicken

Snack: Pita Pizzas

Dinner: Masala Chops

Dessert: Sweet Apples

Day 5:

Breakfast: Hasselback Potatoes

Lunch: Chicken Enchiladas

Snack: Spanakopita Bites

Dinner: Sheet Pan Pork with Apples

Dessert: Bread Pudding

Day 6:

Breakfast: Morning Bagels

Lunch: Korean Chicken Wings

Snack: Pork Dumplings

Dinner: Cauliflower pork casserole

Dessert: Carrot Cake

Day 7:

Breakfast: Egg Avocado Boats

Lunch: Cheesy Chicken Nachos

Snack: Curry Chickpeas

Dinner: Holiday Ham

Dessert: Glazed Donut

Conclusion

If you are a fan of smart cooking, then Ninja Foodi Digital Air Fry Oven is a perfect fit for you. With this new kitchen miracle, you don't need to switch from appliance to appliance to get a variety of delicious meals. Using a single device, you can roast, toast, Air fry, bake and cook much more. If you haven't brought this kitchen bliss to home or you have it but haven't been able to use it to its full potential, then this cookbook is a right pick! With its variety of recipes, divided into sections, you will be able to explore all the cooking functions of this device. Now you can toast fresh bread slices in the morning and bake an irresistible chicken for dinner, all just by using Ninja Foodi Digital Air Fry Oven.

Remember, when you are done cooking with this digital oven, make sure to clean it thoroughly before putting it away. Thankfully the cleaning is quite when it comes to the Ninja Air Fryer ovens, especially when it comes to SP101 because due to its flip design, you can easily make it stand and open the lower power to remove the crumb tray and clean the oven inside out. After every session, the screen will show the "Red" hot sign on the screen until it is cooled. The moment it is cooled down, the screen shows a "Flip" sign, and the Hot sign disappears. Unplug the device carefully to cut off the power supply. Now remove all the removable items from inside the oven that may include the sheet pan, the wire rack, the Air Fryer basket, and crumb tray. Wash these removable items in the dishwasher or using the soapy water. Let them dry to use again. Hold the handle under the lid and flip the oven by pushing its front upward. Pull the base of the oven, and it will come out like the lid. Wipe off the base with the help of a wet cloth. Allow its base to dry out completely, then close it.

So, if you really want to avail all the smart cooking feature offered by this amazing cooking appliance, then it's about time that you adorn your kitchen counter with this smartly designed multipurpose oven, and then start cooking some magic at home using our special Ninja digital Air Fry oven recipe collection.

www.ingramcontent.com/pod-product-compliance
Lightning Source LLC
Chambersburg PA
CBHW080610170426
43209CB00007B/1389